Out of the Ordinary

Refining Academic Reading Skills

Jean Zukowski/Faust

Northern Arizona University

HEINLE & HEINLE
™
THOMSON LEARNING

Australia • Canada • Mexico • Singapore • Spain • United Kingdom • United States

HEINLE & HEINLE
THOMSON LEARNING

Out of the Ordinary
Refining Academic Skills
Jean Zukowski/Faust

Developmental Editor: *Phyllis Dobbins*
Production Editor: *Angela Williams Urquhart*
Marketing Manager: *Katrina Byrd*
Manufacturing Coordinator: *Holly Mason*
Production/Composition: *Real Media Solutions*
Copy Editor: *Dina Forbes, WordPlayers*

Photo Researcher: *Robert Bovasso, Constance Wynn-Smith, Real Media Solutions*
Text Designer: *Elizabeth Geary, Real Media Solutions*
Cover Designer: *Bill Brammer Design*
Printer: *Webcom*

For permission to use material from this text or product, contact us:
Tel   1-800-730-2214
Fax   1-800-730-2215
Web   http://www.thomsonrights.com

Library of Congress Control Number: 2001093102
ISBN: 0-15-506033-3

Photo Credits: Page 1: Top, Christine Wallace; Bottom, ©Helen Lau Running; Page 11: ©Bob Casper/Sarbo; Page 23: AP Photo/Will Kincaid; Page 35: Ryan McVay/PhotoDisc; Page 47: Top, ©Richard T. Nowitz/CORBIS; Bottom, Helen Lau Running; Page 59: ©UAD/Photographer: Christoph Gerigk; Creator: Franck Goddio; Page 71: ©Dr. Hans U. Tschersich; Page 83: Leah J. Smith/Arizona Daily Sun; Page 95: Top, ©Nick Koudis/PhotoDisc; Bottom, David Parker; Page 107: ©Shaun Walker/The Times Standard; Page 119: AP Photo/Adam Nadel; Page 129: Beverly Setlowe/Brown Wolf Public Relations; Page 141: ©Layne Kennedy; Page 153: Michael Keller/West Virginia Division of Culture and History; Page 165: Russel Illig/PhotoDisc; Page 177: Top, ©Joel W. Rogers/CORBIS; Bottom, Made with Mountain High Maps™, Digital Wisdom, Inc.; Page 187: Top, Brenda Ahearn; Bottom, Jean Zukowski/Faust; Page 197: ©Kevin Hong/The Daily World; Page 207: Top, Pedro Perez/The Seattle Times 05/03/00; Bottom, Helen Lau Running; Page 219: Top, Tim Campbell, Age of Sail Program/San Francisco Maritime National Historical Park; Bottom, Steve Danford, Age of Sail Program/San Francisco Maritime National Historical Park

Acknowledgments

Special thanks to Phyllis Dobbins, Carolyn Martin, and Angela Urquhart of Heinle & Heinle; Elizabeth Geary, Robert Bovasso, and Conni Wynn-Smith of Real Media Solutions; Dina Forbes and Jacqueline Flamm of WordPlayers; and the in-home support team of one, my husband John.

Contents

To the Instructor

Out of the Ordinary is a series of readings for the high beginning/low intermediate reader of English about extraordinary people and situations. The topics were selected so that concepts and vocabulary could be recycled, making for a respiraled curriculum and a natural understanding of the words. All the focus words are listed in the back of the book so that teachers can find them easily.

Through the use of this text, teachers of new learners of English language reading will be able to enhance the growth of vocabulary and general understanding. Furthermore, the many exercises that follow each reading will help students increase their ability in reading skills.

How Each Reading Is Structured

Anticipatory Set:

Each of the twenty readings in *Out of the Ordinary* begins with establishing some expectations for the reader and with activating students' background knowledge. A small set of questions (Answer These Questions) immediately precedes the reading, establishing a purpose for reading.

The Readings:

Each reading is between 625 and 850 words in length. The topic, one of current human interest, is developed with people and examples. Most of the focus words are explained in context. Some built-in redundancies help students understand the concepts better.

The Graphic Support:

Photographs and drawings will help students anticipate the content and also extract the meanings of unfamiliar concepts.

Learn the New Words:

The focus words are listed and defined as they exist in the reading. The part of speech (noun, non-count noun, adjective, adverb, verb, and idiom) is also noted.

Practice the New Words:

Sentences that extend the meaning are provided so that the students can practice with the new words. There are also matching exercises and questions about the focus words.

Find the Details:

A series of questions that require discrete information from the students leads them to review the reading.

Give Your Opinion:

In this section, students are asked what they think. These questions can serve as the basis for class discussion.

Make Some Inferences:

The information in the reading can be extended. Students can synthesize answers from the reading by answering the inference questions. By encouraging the critical thought required in making inferences, teachers help students learn to manipulate ideas and encourage interaction with the text.

Find the Main Ideas:

In this part of each lesson, students are asked to weigh the relative importance of ideas. They might be asked to select an appropriate title, to check all the supporting ideas and identify the main idea from a group, or to determine which ideas contribute to the main idea. In a number of different formats, the extraction of the thesis of the reading or a part of the reading is encouraged.

Write Your Thoughts:

Students are given topics for writing in their personal journals or for paragraphs to hand in as homework.

Other Types of Exercises:

In units in which order of occurrence is relevant, students are asked to determine the sequence of events. In other units, there are suggestions for special activities.

How to Use *Out of the Ordinary*

The format of *Out of the Ordinary* allows for great flexibility. Because the text is arranged for recycling of concepts and vocabulary as well as increasing challenge in the exercises, teachers will find it is easiest to use the readings in sequence. However, these readings can be the main focus of a class or can be used as extra readings. Some teachers might prefer to teach some of the vocabulary before students attempt the reading. Others might begin with a discussion of the photographs. Other teachers might read the article aloud to their students as a beginning point, being aware that their students might not understand everything the first time through.

However you choose to use *Out of the Ordinary*, I hope you enjoy using it as much as I have enjoyed writing it.

Jean Zukowski/Faust

Christine's Hogan-and-Breakfast

Christine Wallace's hogan is a traditional Navajo house. It is made of pine poles and faces the east.

These women are weaving a rug.

Prepare to Read

- Do you like to travel?
- How is travel "out of the ordinary" for you?
- What do you learn from travel?
- Do you enjoy new experiences?
- What do you know about Native American people? Where do they live? What do they eat? What do they wear?
- Look at the picture on the first page of this unit. What will you learn about?
- Make a list of your own new words, and try to understand the main ideas.
- What does the title mean to you?

Answer These Questions

First read the story, and then try to answer these questions.

1. Who is Christine Wallace?
2. How is Christine's "hotel" different from other places for tourists?
3. What is Christine selling?
4. Why is it worth $125 a night?
5. What work does Christine have to do for her business?

Read the Story

Christine's Hogan-and-Breakfast

1   A heavy sheepskin covers the door. The door faces east, away from the setting sun. You have to bend down low to pass through it. You step down into a cool room. There are two tiny glass windows. The floor is hard earth. This is your
5   unique hotel room. There is central heat! It's a black half-barrel stove in the middle of your hogan. A stack of twisted wood sits next to the half-barrel stove, ready to give warmth.

There is no real chimney, just a black pipe. It leads up into the top of your octagon wooden structure. The smoke escapes
10   through a hole in the roof. Let's hope for no rain. If it rains, there will be some wet earth in your room. There is nothing to keep the rain out of the smoke hole. If it rains, stay away from the center of the room.

The sides of the structure are made of straight pine poles.
15   Each pole is about seven inches in diameter. These poles were once straight trees on the mountains. These poles make the hogan. Someone stacked and crossed them at each of eight points around the structure. There are ten poles on each of the eight sides. That makes a total of 80 poles. Between the poles
20   there is a mixture of mud and straw, to keep out the high desert plateau winds. The roof is made of wattle, crossed and woven sticks covered and sealed with layers of sun-baked clay. The roof is waterproof except for the center around the smoke hole.

Is there running water in your hogan? Well, there are ten
25   one-gallon plastic water bottles. There is also a green basin on a green table and a green bucket under it. You pour the water into the basin. That is your running water. And you have a choice of places to sleep. There are two twin beds with bright blankets on them. These beds are along two of the eight
30   sides of the hogan. They are for the less adventuresome. Do you want the real experience of a Navajo night of sleep? You can choose a hammock from several hammocks. There are two large hooks for a hammock. There is also a stack of fluffy white sheepskins. Those who are ready to be Navajos
35   for the night choose sheepskins.

Outside the hogan there is a real outhouse. It is the only toilet. Yours is made entirely of wood, and it smells sweet, of mountain herbs. Tonight Christine will leave you with a kerosene lantern. It hangs on a large hook near the door. It

40 serves as a night-light. The lantern is burning, but its wick is turned down to the smallest flame. You will need it to use the outhouse in the night. She shows you how to turn up the wick to light your way.

There is special evening entertainment. Christine's parents
45 and grandparents are traditional Navajos. They live in the old way. They come to sit with you outside by the fire pit. After supper of fry bread and mutton stew, they will tell stories under the stars. The bright stars will light everything through the clear, dry air on a moonless night. They begin to speak in
50 Navajo. Christine translates. They explain the role of corn in Navajo culture. They tell you about the greeting of the sun in the morning. They answer your questions about Navajo life. They supply you with the fine things of Navajo life. There is even some yucca shampoo in a bowl. You can use it with the
55 bottles of water and the green basin.

Christine explains the sounds of the night. You will hear the sound of coyotes in the distance. Those coyotes are unlikely to come near the hogan. They certainly won't come in. There is nothing to fear from coyotes. She smiles and suggests
60 another cultural experience. She can arrange for you to go to a Navajo sweat lodge tomorrow. It is a Native American sauna. Then the family members get up to go to their own hogan. It is close, only a half of a mile deeper in the canyon. They explain about breakfast. It will be blue corn mush and
65 fry bread with honey. It will be ready an hour after dawn. At Christine's hogan-and-breakfast, your hostess can also serve eggs and bacon. There will be coffee, too, black and strong.

Christine's 30-year-old hogan is in a small canyon. It is about ten miles on a dirt track from the Navajo capital
70 of Window Rock, New Mexico. She doesn't advertise for customers. By word of mouth she gets guests four or five

nights a week for her $125-a-night one-room hotel. Many of her guests come from overseas. Most of them stay at least two nights. They might join Christine's brother herding sheep.

75   Others might decide to gather pinion nuts with her during the days. Someone might spend a quiet day with her mother. She is weaving a rug. These tourists learn about the Navajo way of life through experience. They are not the typical tourists. Christine's hogan-and-breakfast place isn't a typical hotel,

80   either. It's out of the ordinary.

Now go back to *Answer These Questions.*

Can you answer the questions? If not, then read the story again and continue the lesson. When you reach the end of the unit, go back to the questions again. Perhaps you will have answers then.

Learn the New Words

Here are some of the new words and meanings in this reading:

1. **adventuresome** (adjective): willing to take risks; liking to try new things
2. a **basin** (noun): a shallow container to hold water; a container to wash things in
3. a **bucket** (noun): a deep container with a handle for carrying water
4. a **chimney** (noun): a tube of brick or metal for smoke from a fire to leave a building
5. a **coyote** (noun): a wild animal of the dog family
6. **diameter** (non-count noun): measurement from one side through the middle to the other side
7. a **dirt track** (noun): a simple road without a special hard surface
8. **fluffy** (adjective): cloud-like
9. a **hammock** (noun): a long, narrow piece of net or cloth with rope at each of two ends, hung on two hooks and used for sleeping

10. a **lantern** (noun): a case for holding a light, usually with fuel-like oil and a lighted burning string, a wick

11. an **octagon** (noun): an eight-sided shape

12. an **outhouse** (noun): a small separate structure (here, for use as a toilet)

13. a **plateau** (noun): a piece of high-level land in the mountains

14. a **sauna** (noun): a type of steam bath popular in Finland

15. a **stack** (noun): a neat pile (of wood, cloth, clothing)

16. a **structure** (noun): a building

17. a **sweat lodge** (noun): a structure for bathing, using steam, like a sauna

18. to **twist** (verb): to bend and make knots in order to make crooked

19. **twisted** (adjective): bent or crooked

20. **unique** (adjective): one-of-a-kind

21. **waterproof** (adjective): covered so that water cannot pass through

22. **wattle** (non-count noun): mixture of mud or clay on sticks, used for building walls

23. a **wick** (count noun): a thick string or cord in a candle or lamp, which takes in oil and burns with a small steady flame

Practice the New Words

Look at the list of new words. Then read these sentences. Use the correct form of a word from the list to fill in each blank. There may be some words that you will use more than once and some that you will not use at all.

1. I have to wash my socks by hand. I need some soap and a

   _____*basin*_____ to wash them in.

2. I have a _____ of warm water for the washing. I carried it from the kitchen.

3. There are no electric lights in the camping place. We will need

   to take a _____ .

4. We are going camping. I'll take along a new _____

   to tie between two trees. I will sleep on it.

5. Navajo people always build a hogan in an _____

   shape.

6. The roof of a hogan is sticks and clay, or _____ ,

   and it is _____ . In other words, it stays dry except

   for the area around the smoke hole.

7. Outside every hogan there is a _____ of wood to

   burn for cooking and for heat.

8. They built a fireplace, but they still need a _____

   for the smoke.

9. There's some lamp oil in the lantern, but the _____

   is very short. The lantern needs a new one.

10. At night on the plateau, you can hear the sounds of the

    _____ in the distance.

11. The road to the hogan is really just a _____ .

12. Yesterday the clouds were dark and black. Today they are

    _____ like sheepskin.

13. This apple is very large, at least four inches in _____ !

14. Navajo land is a high _____ with mountains to the

    the north, south, east, and west.

15. This Navajo rug is _____ . There is no other like it.

16. A Navajo _____ is like a Finnish _____ ;
    water on hot rocks makes steam, and a person can get clean.

17. There is no running water, so there is no toilet or bathtub in the
    house. There is an _____ in the yard, away from
    the house.

18. The road isn't straight. It _____ one way and then
    another.

19. _____ people enjoy taking risks and trying new
    things.

20. A Navajo hogan is an unusual building. It is an eight-sided
    _____ .

Find the Details

Skim and scan to find the answers to these questions.

1. How many pine poles make a hogan?   _____

2. Where do the pine poles come from?   _____

3. What is a typical Navajo supper?   _____

4. What do Navajos usually eat for breakfast?   _____

5. What is a traditional Navajo stove made of?   _____

6. Light comes from several different sources. How many can you
   name? Find five.   _____ _____

   _____ _____ _____

7. What do traditional Navajos use for heat?   _____

8. Yucca is a desert plant. What do traditional Navajos use it for?

   _____

Give Your Opinion

Read these questions. Tell your classmates what you think.

1. Why does the Navajo house face the east? Do you have any ideas?
2. Why is corn important to the Navajos?
3. What differences could there be between a traditional Navajo and an urban (city) Navajo?
4. Sheep are important to the Navajo. Why is this true?
5. The mountains are not close to most Navajo groups. But they travel to the mountains to get one thing. What is it? Why?

Make Some Inferences

Circle all the right answers.

1. Christine probably explains about the sounds in the night because...
   a. she wants to frighten people about the wild animals' sounds at night.
   b. some people might worry about the unusual sounds and be afraid.
   c. people need to know that it is very dangerous to live in a hogan.
   d. city people don't know about the sounds of coyotes.
   e. other tourists were probably afraid and asked her about the sounds.
   f. she doesn't want people to be comfortable in the hogan.

2. The Navajo people use sweat lodges because...
   a. they don't like showers.
   b. they don't have running water in hogans.
   c. they live in a dry climate with not much water.
   d. they like to be clean.
   e. they believe that sweat lodges make a person healthy.
   f. the sweat lodge is how they make hot water.

Find the Main Ideas

Circle the best answer.

1. What is the main idea of Christine's business?

    a. Everyone likes to listen to stories.

    b. Some tourists want to learn from experience.

    c. Every person needs to have a hogan of his or her own.

    d. There are not many hotels near Window Rock, New Mexico.

2. What is the main idea of a stay in a hogan for two days?

    a. to learn about the Navajo way of life

    b. to become a sheep-herder

    c. to eat traditional Navajo food

    d. to understand the importance of sheep to the Navajos

3. What is the main idea of a hogan?

    a. It must have glass windows for air and light.

    b. It must be large and square.

    c. It must be waterproof.

    d. It must be a comfortable place to live.

4. What is the main idea of the reading?

    a. Typical tourists do not stay in hogans in Window Rock, New Mexico.

    b. A half-barrel stove can provide central heat.

    c. Staying at Christine's hogan is an educational experience.

    d. Most tourists want to have a unique experience.

Write Your Thoughts

1. What is a traditional person? How does a traditional person keep the culture of a group? Is culture important? Why or why not?

2. What is extraordinary about Christine's place for tourists? Does anyone think that her hogan-and-breakfast is ordinary? (Who would?)

2 The Stairs in the Chapel

These stairs form two complete circles, have no central support, and were made without nails from a rare hardwood.

Prepare to Read

- Think about the buildings near your home. Are they beautiful? Why are some buildings more beautiful than others?
- The job of a carpenter is to work with wood and make things from it. What tools does a carpenter usually have? Which ones are necessary?
- Each person is unique; there is no one else in the whole world exactly like another person. What other unique things can you think of?
- Look at the picture on the first page of this unit. What will you learn about?
- Make a list of your own new words, and try to understand the main ideas.
- Do you get any ideas from the title?

Answer These Questions

First read the story, and then try to answer these questions.

1. Where is the chapel?
2. What is unique about the chapel?
3. What are nuns?
4. What is faith?

Read the Story

The Stairs in the Chapel

1   Santa Fe, New Mexico, is a small mountain city that has a long and interesting history and a strong Spanish heritage. The city's name means "Holy Faith." It reflects the belief of the people in God. There is a convent there. The nuns who
5   live there are called the Sisters of Loretto. There is a small church, a chapel, next to the convent on a back street near the center of the city. It was built in 1822 by a French bishop, Bishop Lamy. He wanted a church like the beautiful churches

of his native France. The small Gothic structure was unique
10　　in Southwestern America, where the Mexican style of adobe
building was common. The bishop ordered plans for the
building from France. And the workers began the building.

　　　The little church is 25 feet wide, 75 feet long, and 85 feet
high. Light streams in through beautiful windows of stained
15　　glass. One of these windows is high on the wall above the
back of the church, in the choir loft, which is 22 feet above
the floor. The balance of the design made the building truly
a work of art.

　　　The carpenters had nearly finished the construction of
20　　the chapel when someone noticed a big mistake. The chapel
was lovely, and so was the choir loft. However, there was no
way for a person to get up to the choir loft (where the pipe
organ and singers would be) except by climbing up the
carpenters' ladders.

25　　　The architect had forgotten to plan a staircase! The Sisters
of Loretto called in many carpenters to ask for suggestions.
Each carpenter said that a 22-foot staircase in the available
space was simply not possible. They wanted to tear down
the choir loft and begin again. The nuns didn't have the
30　　money for such a job. Furthermore, they didn't want to
destroy the beauty of the design. As women with a strong
belief in God, they began to pray for an answer. They prayed
a nine-day prayer, called a novena. They asked St. Joseph,
who was a carpenter himself, for help.

35　　　According to the legend, on the ninth day of their prayers,
a man came to the convent. He had nothing but a donkey and
a simple toolbox. He was looking for work. Two of the nuns
took him to the chapel. They showed him the problem with
the choir loft. They asked if he could build a staircase. He said
40　　that he could. So they hired him.

The old carpenter opened the toolbox and took out only three tools. He had a hammer, a saw, and a T square. He began to work. He worked steadily for several months. At one point, he asked the nuns for a tub of water. They saw

45   him put pieces of wood into the tub to soak. But he asked for very little else. He simply worked on quietly. Then one day, months later, the man disappeared. He had gone without any pay and without getting even a word of thanks. The nuns went into the chapel and found the staircase. It was finished,

50   but the carpenter wasn't there.

    The staircase that he built is magnificent. It is a 22-foot spiral, with two 360-degree turns in it. There are 33 steps in the two full circles of the spiral. There is no center support. In fact, no one knows why it stands up at all. There are no

55   nails in the entire staircase! The carpenter used wooden pegs instead of metal nails. Another mystery is the supplies for the building. No one knows where the carpenter got his wood. There were no bills from local lumberyards for wood. all the owners said he had not come to them for lumber. No one

60   could tell where the wood came from. Furthermore, the wood is unusual. It is a rare type of wood that does not grow in the southwest region.

    The nuns wanted to pay the man for his work and for the wood, but he was never seen again. They tried to find him.

65   They put an advertisement in the local newspaper and in the newspapers of Albuquerque, the biggest city in the area. No one answered the ad. No one knew who the carpenter was or where he went.

    These two great mysteries about the spiral staircase in

70   the Loretto chapel remain without answers. Even today, no

one knows the identity of the carpenter who built it. No one can explain the miracle of the staircase construction. Some people say that the carpenter was St. Joseph himself.

Now go back to *Answer These Questions.*

Can you answer the questions? If not, then read the story again and continue the lesson. When you reach the end of the unit, go back to the questions again. Perhaps you will have answers then.

Learn the New Words

Here are some of the new words and meanings in this reading.

1. an **architect** (noun): a person who plans buildings
2. a **carpenter** (noun): a person who makes things out of wood
3. a **choir loft** (noun): a raised space over a floor and under a roof in a church, where musicians usually sit
4. a **convent** (noun): a home for nuns
5. **faith** (non-count noun): belief (as faith in God)
6. a **hammer** (noun): a tool with a heavy metal head and a wooden handle, used to pound nails into wood
7. **heritage** (non-count noun): cultural tradition
8. an **identity** (noun): who someone is; a name
9. a **ladder** (noun): a device of two poles with pieces across like steps on which a person can climb to a higher level
10. **lumber** (non-count noun): wood that is cut for building
11. **magnificent** (adjective): grand; majestic; beautiful
12. a **miracle** (noun): an extraordinary thing or happening
13. a **mystery** (noun): a puzzling event
14. **one's native country** (noun): one's home country
15. a **novena** (noun): a prayer, part of which is said every day for nine days

16. a **peg** (noun): a small piece of wood that is pounded into a hole through two pieces of wood to hold them together; a wedge-shaped piece of wood; any piece of wood with that shape

17. a **prayer** (noun): a humble and sincere request to God for help

18. **rare** (adjective): unusual; not often seen

19. a **saw** (noun): a tool with sharp metal teeth on it, used to cut wood into pieces

20. a **spiral** (noun): a shape made with a point in the middle and a line with an ever-increasing diameter

21. a **T square** (noun): a tool used to make and measure angles before cutting wood

22. a **tub** (noun): a large container for holding water, usually with no handles or two handles

Practice the New Words

A. Draw a line between the two words or phrases with similar meanings (not exactly the same meanings).

1. faith	a. destroy
2. nuns	b. plan
3. church	c. belief
4. building	d. stairs
5. building	e. job
6. ladder	f. structure
7. peg	g. sisters
8. architect	h. chapel
9. steps	i. wood for building
10. prayer	j. unusual
11. design	k. beautiful
12. lovely	l. nail
13. work	m. construction
14. rare	n. carpenter
15. tear down	o. staircase
16. lumber	p. novena

B. Look at the list of new words. Then read these sentences. Use the correct form of a word from the list to fill in each blank. There may be some words that you will use more than once and some that you will not use at all.

1. The stamp collectors look forward to the stamp show because they will see some _____ stamps.

2. This building was designed by a famous _____ . His sense of style and balance are unique, so people know his work as soon as they see it.

3. All the people in the choir went to the _____ .

4. The father of the children said a _____ each night for a job because he wanted to be able to take care of his children.

5. The dancers moved in a large circle, from the center of the room out toward the walls, in a great _____ .

6. Who is the _____ who made this beautiful table? It is truly a work of art!

7. Part of the tradition of a Mexican family in our neighborhood is to say a _____ every year during the first nine days of June. The family gathers each evening to pray together.

8. Such family gatherings are a traditional part of their Spanish _____ .

9. There is a kitten in the tall tree in the backyard. We need a _____ to help the kitten get down safely.

10. I want to hang a picture in this room. I have a nail, but I still need a _____ .

11. There is a twenty-dollar bill on the table. No one knows where that money came from! It's a great _____ to us all.

12. No one knows the _____ of the person who put the money there.

13. The woman was very ill, but then suddenly she was healthy. The doctor said it was a _____ .

14. A builder commonly uses some simple tools in construction; among them is a tool for making straight lines and corners. It is called a _____ .

15. The people cut wood for their campfire with a small

_____ .

16. The view from the top of the mountain was _____ .

17. They put hot water in a _____ to wash their clothing.

18. Belief in oneself and in one's ability to learn is an important part of adult education. It's not always easy to have such

_____ in oneself.

19. The staircase had no nails in it, only wooden _____ .

20. None of the nuns were hurt in the fire that destroyed their home, but they had to build a new _____ .

21. The builders bought the wood for the house at the local

_____ yard.

Find the Details

Skim and scan to find the answers to these questions.

1. When was the chapel built? _____

2. Where was Bishop Lamy from? _____

3. Where is the choir loft? _____

4. What is the meaning of Santa Fe? _____

5. What kind of windows does the chapel have?

   _____

6. What tools did the carpenter use? _____

7. What is the shape of the Loretto staircase? _____

8. How high is the Loretto chapel? _____

9. Where do nuns live? _____

10. How many steps are there to the staircase? _____

11. What kind of wood did the carpenter use for the staircase?

    _____

12. What is Albuquerque? _____

 Give Your Opinion

Read these questions. Tell your classmates what you think.

1. Every year thousands of tourists come to Santa Fe, and most of them go to the Loretto Chapel. Why do people come to the chapel?

2. Why do you think that Bishop Lamy wanted a Gothic chapel?

3. Why is it easier to build a spiral staircase with a center pole for support?

4. Why was the chapel made without stairs to the choir loft?

5. Why did the Sisters of Loretto want to find the carpenter?

6. Why do you think the Sisters of Loretto couldn't find the carpenter?

7. What is "old-fashioned" about the staircase?

Make Some Inferences

Read these questions and think about them. Then answer them.

1. If no one in Santa Fe sold wood to the carpenter, where did he get the wood for the staircase? _____

2. Why did the carpenter need a tub? _____

3. How many degrees are there in a full circle?

   _____

4. Why did the other carpenters say that it was not possible to build a staircase to the loft? _____

5. Why do some people say that St. Joseph came to build the staircase? _____

6. What makes the Loretto chapel staircase unique in all the world?

   _____

 Find the Main Ideas

Circle the best answer.

1. What is the main idea of the problem with the chapel?
   a. There was a mistake in the plans.
   b. The architect wasn't really French.
   c. The carpenters could not follow the plans.
   d. The design for the chapel was beautiful.

2. What is the main idea of the way the nuns solved the problem?
   a. They looked for a carpenter until they found one.
   b. They decided to build a staircase themselves.
   c. Two of them wanted to use a ladder to climb up to the choir loft.
   d. They were women of great faith who prayed for an answer.

3. What is the main idea of the reading?

   a. There is a magnificent staircase in Santa Fe's Loretto Chapel.

   b. A mysterious carpenter built a miracle of a staircase.

   c. The bishop who wanted the chapel was from France.

   d. The choir loft was 22 feet high.

Write Your Thoughts

1. What are your thoughts about the old carpenter? Who was he? Why did he come?

2. What unusual things have happened to you? How can you explain them?

3. The Sisters of Loretto prayed for an answer to the choir loft problem. What other ways do people use to find solutions to problems?

3 Modern Cattle Rustlers

The Egly family are modern cattle ranchers.

Prepare to Read

- One of the rules of society says, "No stealing." Why is this an important rule?
- What do you know about the Great Plains?
- What do you know about cowboys? What is their job? How do modern cowboys move from place to place?
- What are most cowboy movies about?

Answer These Questions

First read the story, and then try to answer these questions.

1. What is the problem that most cattle ranchers face today?
2. What is a cattle rancher's merchandise?
3. What tool is used in branding?
4. Why does Colorado have a brands inspector?

Read the Story

Modern Cattle Rustlers

1   How do you keep someone from stealing your belongings? One answer is to lock them up. Another answer is to put a mark on them. Then others will know that they are yours. Both ways have worked for years.

5   On the great grasslands of North America, ranchers raise cattle. The land of the Great Plains stretches from Mexico and Texas in the south to Saskatchewan in the north. Some of the land is too dry to raise crops. However, the thick natural grass of the plains is good food for animals. Much of the

10   land belongs to national governments. Ranchers pay their governments for "grazing rights." In other words, they pay for each cow that grazes on the national land.

The cattle roam on the "free range" and eat all the grass they want. The grasslands are free of fences, not free of cost.

15　Furthermore, the cows have to wander over many acres to
find enough food. Therefore, the cows from one ranch can be
scattered over many miles of plains. How does one rancher
recognize his cows? He uses a brand. A simple branding
system marks cows. Each mature cow (though not every
20　young calf) has a "brand" on it. A branding iron (hot metal)
burns a scar on the tough cowhide (skin). According to the
law, a cattle buyer for a meatpacking company can buy only
cows with brands. This branding system is over 200 years
old, and for years, it has worked well. Unfortunately, times
25　have changed.

Many movies about the Old West were made about cattle
rustlers. These thieves took the cattle and sold them. Some
people don't know about it, but there are cattle rustlers
today, too. After all, cows are worth a lot of money, each one
30　between $500 and $1,000. And ranchers' cattle are out in the
open, on the range. Some owners don't see their cattle for
months. Gary Shoun, a Colorado brand inspector, sums up
the problem. "You don't see other business owners leave a
piece of valuable merchandise up on the side of a mountain.
35　We cattle ranchers are the only industry in the world that has
to do business that way." What does he mean? He means that
cattle on the open range are vulnerable. They are in danger of
being stolen. Someone can simply take them.

In the movies, the cattle rustlers came in at night and
40　rounded up the cattle. They then "drove" the cattle away
from the land. Cowboys and dogs moved the herd away from
the land of the owner. Sometimes the owner was able to see
the stealing. Sometimes a rancher was able to stop the
rustlers from taking the cattle.

45　Today's cattle rustlers use modern methods. They use
airplanes, motorcycles, and dogs to circle the cows. They

drive huge trucks out onto the land. The cattle are put into the trucks, and no one even sees them. These modern rustlers have special equipment. For example, they carry collapsible

50   fences. They can put up and take down these fences in minutes. They use the airplanes to find cattle. Then with dogs and motorcycles, they drive the cattle to a central place. They load the cattle onto closed trucks and drive away.

The Egly family has a cattle ranch in North Dakota. They

55   buy grazing rights from the National Grasslands. In one spring, they lost about 150 cows. They own their ranch land, but they are worried. Can they continue if they lose so much in one year? They cannot afford such great losses.

Another rancher, Gene Fedorenko, lost a total of 100

60   animals. The rustlers cut the fences on his land. They drove their trucks in and took the cattle away. He found tire tracks from heavy trucks. Fedorenko figures his loss at $40,000.

The price of beef is high. Therefore, there is an increase in stealing. It's not easy for a rancher to know exactly how

65   many cows he owns. Rustlers steal some. Furthermore, some cows simply wander off. That makes it hard to know how many cows are missing. One thing is clear: there is more rustling. Another fact is this: modern rustlers use modern techniques. They use radios and even satellite communication.

70   Officials are thinking about ways to fight the rustlers and protect rancher's cows. Some new strategies include DNA testing and computer chips on cows' ears. The branding system worked well for years, but it isn't enough anymore.

Now go back to *Answer These Questions.*

Can you answer the questions? If not, then read the story again and continue the lesson. Go back to the questions at the end of the unit. Perhaps you will have answers then.

 Learn the New Words

Here are some of the new words and meanings in this reading.

1. **belongings** (plural noun): personal property; what one owns
2. to **be worth** (idiom): to have the value of
3. **collapsible** (adjective): fold-up (able to be made smaller to carry by folding up into a small package)
4. **DNA testing** (non-count noun): a scientific way to identify animals
5. to **drive cattle** (idiom): to cause cattle to move toward a certain place
6. to **graze** (verb): to eat grass off the land
7. a **herd** (noun): a group of cattle or sheep
8. a **hide** (noun): the thick skin of an animal
9. an **inspector** (noun): a government person who checks on things
10. **mature** (adjective): full-grown; adult
11. **merchandise** (non-count noun): goods to sell
12. **out in the open** (idiom): to live outdoors without protection
13. to **raise cattle** (idiom): to take care of animals so that they can be sold
14. to **roam** (verb): to go freely and without direction
15. to **round up** (verb) to gather; to collect
16. a **rustler** (noun): a cattle thief
17. **satellite communication** (noun): connections like cell telephones that use satellites above the Earth
18. to **stretch** (verb): to extend from one place to another; to cover all the space between two limits
19. to **sum up** (idiom): to make a general statement about

20. **vulnerable** (adjective): not protected; open to attack
21. to **wander** (verb): to walk without direction

Practice the New Words

A. Look at the list of new words. Then read these sentences. Use the correct form of a word from the list to fill in each blank. There may be some words that you will use more than once and some that you will not use at all.

1. If a store has a variety of _____ , the customers will be happy because they will be able to choose what they want.

2. The beef inspectors found some cows that _____ had stolen from a rancher.

3. Baby birds stay in the nest, and their parents go to look for food. The babies are _____ while their parents are gone.

4. I haven't seen that movie, but I read about it. The review _____ the story.

5. That movie is not for children, but it is probably O.K. for _____ people.

6. The cowboys' job was to _____ to market without losing any of the cows.

7. Cow _____ was made into shoes and belts.

8. Modern cattle thieves use motorcycles and dogs to _____ the cattle.

9. In South America, there are great grasslands that

    _____ from the Andes Mountains to the

    Atlantic Ocean.

10. There are no fences on the open range, so the cattle can

    _____ over large areas.

11. The people saw a _____ of hundreds of

    cattle.

12. Cattle ranchers need the grass of the Great Plans to be able

    to _____ for money.

13. Cell phones work because of _____ .

14. It is easy, but not cheap, to identify a person by

    _____ .

15. I found my book in the backyard after the rain. I'll never

    leave a book _____ again.

16. Campers use _____ equipment. They can put

    it up and take it down quickly.

17. One cow _____ between $500 and $1,000.

18. I packed everything that I own into three boxes. Those boxes

    had all my _____ in them.

19. In the spring, cattle like to _____ close to

    roads because of the new grass.

20. The state government has _____ to check on

    brands of cows on the open range.

21. All year long the cattle _____ on the open
    range, but once a year the ranchers collect them, sell some,
    and brand the calves.

B. Draw a line between the two words or phrases with similar
    meanings.

1. roam	a. eat grass
2. unprotected	b. merchandise
3. herd	c. make a general statement
4. gather	d. mature
5. adult	e. wander
6. things for sale	f. round up
7. sum up	g. vulnerable
8. graze	h. group

Find the Details

Skim and scan to find the answers to these questions.

1. What are the names of two ranching families in the reading?

    _____ _____

2. How old is the branding system? _____

3. What is a collapsible fence? _____

4. According to the law, if a cattle-buyer want to buy a cow, what
   is every cow supposed to have? _____

5. Modern cowboys don't use horses very much. What do they use
   instead? _____

6. How were Gene Fedorenko's cattle taken from him?

    _____

7. Who buys cattle? _____

8. What are some modern methods that cattle thieves use?

   _____

9. Who is Gary Shoun?   _____

10. Who owns the National Grasslands?   _____

 Give Your Opinion

Read these questions. Tell your classmates what you think.

1. Do you think computer chips on cows' ears could stop cattle rustling?
2. Do you think fences would help the problem? Why or why not?
3. How can cattle rustlers sell the cows that they steal?

 Find the Main Ideas

Circle the best answer.

1. The main idea of cattle rustling is…
   a. keeping animals safe from thieves.
   b. buying grazing rights from the government.
   c. taking someone else's belongings for the money.
   d. finding cows that are missing.

2. The main idea of branding is…
   a. finding the new young calves.
   b. marking cows to identify them.
   c. selling cows to meatpacking companies.
   d. for the inspectors.

3. The main idea of the reading is…
   a. that stealing cows is part of the Old West, like in the movies.
   b. that the problem of cattle rustling is over.
   c. that cattle ranchers are using satellites to find their animals.
   d. that the branding system is not stopping cattle rustling.

Make Some Inferences

Circle the best answer.

1. Why do some calves not have brands?
   a. They are too young for brands.
   b. No one knows whose calves they are.
   c. They run away to avoid brands.
   d. They belong to the government.

2. How do you know that Fedorenko's stolen cattle included many calves?
   a. It is in the reading.
   b. Fedorenko saw their tracks on the ground by the fences.
   c. He didn't really know how many cattle there were.
   d. Mature cows are worth more than $400 each.

3. Why do cattle roam over such a large area?
   a. The cows like to roam.
   b. The cows look for good grass over a large area.
   c. The cows like the mountains.
   d. The cows don't have cowboys watching them, so they wander.

4. What is "free" about the "free range"?
   a. It doesn't cost anything.
   b. It doesn't belong to anyone.
   c. It doesn't have fences.
   d. It doesn't have grass on it.

5. Why is it important to rustlers to be fast in taking the cattle?
   a. They have to find the cows.
   b. Slow rustlers are caught.
   c. Inspectors are watching them.
   d. The cattle will run away.

6. Why don't ranchers grow crops as food to sell on their land?

   a. They like animals better.

   b. The land is too dry for growing crops.

   c. They are too far from places to sell crops.

   d. They cannot buy farming rights.

7. How many cows do you think the Eglys own if they are worried about losing 150 cows?

   a. about 200

   b. about 300

   c. about 1,000

   d. about a million

8. Why don't ranchers lock up their cows to keep them safe?

   a. Cows hate fences.

   b. Cowboys hate fences.

   c. A cow needs a large area to graze.

   d. The open range has no fences.

Write Your Thoughts

1. Think about the vulnerable cattle on the open range. Why are they so vulnerable?

2. Why do you think some people steal?

4 As You Smell It

One of the most important smells is the smell of food.

Prepare to Read

Think about the work of a nose.

- What smells do you like?
- What smells are not pleasant?
- Look at the picture on the first page of this unit. What will you learn about?
- Make a list of your own new words, and try to understand the main ideas.
- Do you get any ideas from the title?

Answer These Questions

First read the story, and then try to answer these questions.

1. What job does the watery mucus do in your nose?
2. How does a smell travel through the air?
3. How is a human nose like a filter?

Read the Story

As You Smell It

1   Everyone has a nose, but very few people stop to think about the work that a nose does. Your nose is easy to see because it sits in the middle of your face right between your eyes. You may think that your nose is nice-looking or ugly,
5   but it is always important. Furthermore, your nose does two important jobs for you—three if you wear glasses. Its first main job is part of breathing. Of course, your nose takes in air, but it also cleans the air. There is some natural wetness inside of every person's nose. This thick liquid in a nose is
10   called mucus. The liquid mucus is on hairs in the nose. The mucus catches little particles and holds them, removing them from the air. Therefore, those little particles (dirt) are

prevented from getting into the lungs, where they could cause damage. Clean air is available for the lungs. When a person

15   blows her nose, then the particles come out with the mucus.

The second job for your nose is to smell for you. Just think about it for a moment: smell is an important sense. Smell is often the first warning of something dangerous. For example, think of the smell of food. A pleasant smell whets

20   your appetite and makes you ready to eat. A foul food smell is a clear signal to stay away from the food. Bad-smelling food can be dangerous to eat. This statement is not always true, however. Some cheese smells bad, but it tastes delicious!

It is interesting to investigate how a nose works. How

25   does a nose smell an apple, for example? An apple gives off some chemicals into the air. That air comes into the nose as a gas. The smell of the chemicals comes with the air. In the back of a nose is a small area of tissue. It contains millions of nerves. There are tiny hairs in this area, not like the ones in

30   the front of your nose. These tiny hairs are the "cilia." These cilia have a thin watery mucus on them. The gas (air) comes into the nose. The air passes by the mucus and is dissolved in the mucus. That is how the gas comes into contact with the cilia. The cilia pick up the smell and send it to the brain,

35   where the smell is analyzed and interpreted. (The brain says, "Oh, it's an apple.")

Another funny thing happens in the brain at that moment. The brain remembers the smell in a picture of the past. Smells cause memories to return. Some people respond emotionally

40   to smells because of the thoughts that come to their minds with a smell. They smell a pine tree; they think of Christmas. They smell apples cooking and remember a particular party or a childhood memory of apple pies. They smell peanut butter and remember being in school and eating peanut

45 butter sandwiches for lunch. In other words, smells cause many reactions. The brain's smell-memory connection is an interesting phenomenon.

   Among some animals, smell plays a different role from its role among people. Ants use smell to mark a path to food.
50 Female butterflies attract male butterflies with a smell. And worker bees respond to the smell of the queen bee. Scientists have studied how people respond to smells too. How does the smell of a person affect others? By studying this important question, scientists have learned a lot about human beings.
55 For example, they have uncovered one of the reasons that two people fall in love: They smell good to each other!

   How many smells are there? There are tens of thousands of different smells. Furthermore, some people can tell them all apart. It takes time to train one's eyes to see differences.
60 In the same way, a person can learn to be a good smeller. It just takes practice.

   There is one other interesting fact about human noses. They continue to grow. A baby's nose is very small, and adults' noses are much bigger. A baby's feet are tiny, and
65 adults' feet are much bigger. However, feet stop growing, but many people's noses (and ears) don't stop growing! They get larger and larger. Perhaps our need for air and the sense of smell keep on increasing too.

Now go back to *Answer These Questions.*

Can you answer the questions? If not, then read the story again and continue the lesson. Go back to the questions at the end of the unit. Perhaps you will have answers then.

Learn the New Words

Here are some of the new words and meanings in this reading.

1. to **analyze** (verb): to look at carefully in order to understand well
2. to **attract** (verb): to pull (something toward oneself); to be inviting to
3. to **dissolve** (verb): to become part of a liquid
4. **emotionally** (adverb): with great feeling
5. a **filter** (noun): a screen; a tool to remove impurities
6. **foul** (adjective): bad-smelling
7. to **investigate** (verb): to look into; to ask questions about
8. **lungs** (plural noun): body organ for breathing
9. **mucus** (non-count noun): body liquid from the nose
10. **nerves** (plural noun): receivers for the brain
11. a **particle** (noun): a small bit
12. a **phenomenon** (noun): an event or an interesting happening
13. a **reaction** (noun): an effect caused by something else; a response
14. to **respond** (verb): to give an answer
15. a **role** (noun): a part in a play
16. a **sense** (noun): one of a person's natural ways of understanding information (seeing, smelling, tasting, hearing, feeling)
17. to **take in** (verb): to breathe in; to accept
18. to **train** (verb): to learn how to do something
19. **wetness** (non-count noun): moisture; dampness
20. to **whet** (verb): to sharpen

Practice the New Words

A. Look at the list of new words. Then read these sentences. Use the correct form of a word from the list to fill in each blank. There may be some words that you will use more than once and some that you will not use at all.

1. An automobile needs a _____ for the air so that the air will be clean in the motor.

2. When a person's _____ fill up with water, the person is in serious danger! He or she will not be able to breathe.

3. Three of the young women have decided to _____ to become doctors.

4. My right eye is red and watery because a _____ of dust flew into it.

5. For my homework, I have some information to _____ . I need to understand it well to write a report.

6. There was a serious accident, and the police will have to _____ the cause of it.

7. The _____ in the nose serves some very important purposes.

8. What is that delicious smell? It is _____ my appetite!

9. Have you seen the birds near the flowers? I wonder whether it is the smell of the color that _____ them.

10. If you _____ some honey in apple cider vinegar, you will get a healthful drink. It will taste like apple juice.

11. Plants like damp soil to grow in, but the amount of
    _____ should not stop the roots from breathing.

12. Close the refrigerator door! There's a _____
    smell in there!

13. When a person is hurt, the _____ in the skin
    carry the message to the brain.

14. She was angry about the accident, and she _____
    to the accident by crying.

15. In other words, she acted very _____ .

16. A rainbow is a natural _____ .

17. A mother plays many _____ in her children's
    lives. She takes care of them, she supports them, and she is a
    friend.

18. There is an office at the library where they _____
    books from borrowers.

19. Most people think the most important _____
    is the ability to see.

20. He ate some fruit and got sick. The doctor thinks it was a
    _____ to bad food.

B. Draw a line between the two words or phrases with similar
meanings.

1. bad-smelling	a.	nose
2. lungs	b.	mind
3. female	c.	a chemical in the air
4. respond	d.	foul
5. mark	e.	work
6. male	f.	signal
7. taste	g.	react
8. brain	h.	smell
9. job	i.	man
10. gas	j.	queen

Figure Out the Sequence

What happens next? In the blank in front of each sentence, write a
number between 2 and 10 to show what happens next.

a. _____ The gas travels through the air.

b. _____ Your brain tells you that it smelled an apple.

c. _____ The air with the apple gas passes by the cilia.

d. __*1*__ Someone puts an apple on the table.

e. _____ The cilia send the smell message to your brain.

f. _____ You look around for an apple and find one on the table.

g. _____ Your nose takes in some air with the smell of the apple
in it.

h. _____ Your appetite is whetted by the delicious smell.

i. _____ The apple gives off some chemicals as a gas.

j. _____ The mucus on the cilia dissolves the gas.

Find the Details

Skim and scan to find the answers to these questions.

1. How do ants mark a path to food? _____

2. Which bee has the strongest smell? _____

3. What makes the inside of a human nose wet? _____

4. What foul-smelling food is good to eat? _____

5. What is true about most foul-smelling food? _____

6. How do we smell an apple? _____

7. Where are cilia? _____

8. What reason do scientists give for two people falling in love?

_____

9. How many different kinds of smells are there? _____

10. What reason can there be for the fact that the nose continues to
   grow? _____

Give Your Opinion

Read these questions. Tell your classmates what you think.

1. Which of the five senses do you think is the most important? Why?
2. What do you think of when you smell flowers?
3. What smells do you like and dislike? Why?

Do a Class Activity

With your class, brainstorm a list of twenty smells. Make sure that
each one is very different from the others! Then make two lists:
Pleasant Smells and Foul Smells. Arrange the smells, most (pleasant
or foul) to least (pleasant or foul).

Here are a few ideas to start with: fresh bread, dirty socks, garden
soil, bath water, pickles, spoiled fruit, garbage.

Make Some Inferences

Read these questions and think about them. Then answer them.

1. Why does a human nose have two different kinds of mucus in it?

   _____

2. Why do smells cause emotional responses? _____

3. Why does a queen bee need a special smell? _____

4. Which bees have the best sense of smell? _____

5. Why is a nose especially important to a person who wears glasses?

   _____

6. How can a good sense of smell protect a person?

   _____

 Find the Main Ideas

Circle the best answer.

1. What is the main idea in the first paragraph?
   a. Noses do important work for their owners.
   b. Particles cannot go into the lungs.
   c. The most important job for a nose is to breathe.
   d. Noses have different kinds of mucus.

2. What is the main idea about the reason for bad smell?
   a. Some foods always smell bad.
   b. A bad smell may be a warning.
   c. You should throw away bad-smelling things.
   d. Tiny hairs in the back of a nose pick up smells.

3. What is the main idea about the smell-memory connection in the brain?

   a. It's a natural phenomenon that smells cause memories to return.
   b. The brain doesn't like many smells, and it is likely to make a person sick.
   c. The brain can understand only a few smells.
   d. There are millions of different smells that the brain can understand.

4. What is the main idea of this whole reading?

   a. The human nose continues to grow.
   b. A person's nose does some important work for the person.
   c. A person needs a nose to wear eyeglasses.
   d. Babies' feet stop growing when they are adults.

Write Your Thoughts

1. Do you believe that people fall in love because of their senses of smell? Why or why not?

2. What smells make you think of something special?

3. Is there one smell that you like but most other people do not? What is it? Do you know why it smells good to you?

5 Sky Stone

Turquoise comes in several different shades of blue and green. It can be made into many lovely things.

The silversmith is an artist who works with silver and stones such as turquoise to make beautiful jewelry.

Prepare to Read

- Look at the picture on the first page of this unit. What does it tell you about this story?
- What part of the world do you think of when you see the picture?
- What is a mine? Why do people dig into the earth?

What ideas do you think will be in this unit? Circle those ideas in this list of words.

animals	stone	rock	travel	automobiles
clothing	miners	art	stars	students
camping	Mexico	gold	school	Native Americans

Answer These Questions

First read the story, and then try to answer these questions.

1. What is turquoise?
2. Where do people find turquoise?
3. What do people use turquoise for?
4. What are some unusual things about turquoise?

Read the Story

Sky Stone

1   What does the word *turquoise* make you think of? Ask this question and you'll get a variety of answers. Some will say a green-blue color. Others will say a blue stone. They might mention silver and turquoise jewelry. Experts on the

5   mineral might mention different kinds of turquoise. Some turquoise is bright pure sky blue. Some turquoise has veins of black running through it. Some turquoise is quite dark. You will get many different answers.

People commonly connect turquoise with Native
10   American arts. For example, you can find turquoise jewelry in
the American Southwest. (That is Arizona, New Mexico, and
parts of Colorado, Nevada, and Texas). There are a number of
Native American tribes in these states. They are famous for
silver and turquoise work. They create beautiful rings, belt
15   buckles, necklaces, and combs. Native American silver and
turquoise traditions are strong. Some Navajo and Hopi artists
are famous all over the world. The exquisite detail of their
work is extraordinary. They are truly artists.

On the other hand, there are things that people don't
20   know about turquoise. For example, many people don't know
where it comes from. They do not realize that there were no
true turquoise mines at first. Most of the first sky blue stones
came from the rubble from mines, called tailings. These
rocks were the throw-away rocks of rich copper and silver
25   ores in the mountains of the dry Southwest. Early prospectors,
people looking for mineral wealth, wanted gold. Gold was
the most precious metal. That's why they looked for gold.
The Southwestern mountains had a lot of gold. However,
gold comes in small amounts. These miners found small
30   pieces of gold with silver, copper, and turquoise. These ores
contained many minerals. At first miners didn't recognize the
beauty or value of the blue rock. They didn't know that it
could be polished. They didn't know that it could be shaped
into gemstones. Therefore, they simply threw it away. The blue
35   rocks were among the rocks of copper and silver ore. The piles
of rubble had no value to miners. The native people knew
better. They searched through the tailings. They collected the
stones and polished them. The stone came alive with bright
color. They had gemstones the color of the sky.

40   Today's miners know better too. They don't throw away
chunks of raw turquoise. They even dig for turquoise.
Modern miners burrow into ore seams, the layers in the earth
containing precious metals. Simultaneously they watch for
rich layers or lines in the ore. There are signs that point to
45   the valuable stone. Their main object may be copper and silver
(and any gold that comes their way). However, they look for
the turquoise stone at the same time.

Another rather unknown fact about turquoise is the reason
for the color. The blue comes from copper. Have you ever
50   seen a chunk of copper sulfate $(CuSO_4)$? If you have, you will
remember the sharp clear blue of the mineral. Turquoise is
not all copper. Its chemical composition is mostly a kind of
aluminum phosphate. However, the amount of copper in a
rock determines the richness of the blue. The black lines of
55   some stones are actually silver, silver oxide. Like tiny spider
webs or lines on a road map, these lines can cover a smoothly
polished turquoise surface.

Miners find turquoise only in a few regions of the world.
The area must be dry. And in the distant past, there had to be
60   volcanic activity there. The heat of volcanoes makes turquoise.
The mountains of Iran and Tibet and the American Southwest
fit this description. Those are the places where turquoise is
found today.

Turquoise is the French word for Turkish. However,
65   turquoise stone does not come from Turkey. What is *Turkish*
about *turquoise*? There are two theories. One is that the blue
stone came to Europe through Turkey from Iran. Another
answer is its color. Turkish artists developed a color for glaze
on pottery similar to the stone. The gem took its name from
70   the Turkish color.

There is another truly surprising thing. Few people connect *Turkish* and *turquoise*. Did you think of Turkey when you heard *turquoise*? They are the same word. They are just from two different languages.

 ## Now go back to *Answer These Questions.*

Can you answer the questions? If not, then read the story again and continue the lesson. Go back to the questions at the end of the unit. Perhaps you will have answers then.

 ## Learn the New Words

Here are some of the new words and meanings in this reading.

1. an **artist** (noun): a person who has great ability to make beautiful objects, create music, and the like
2. to **burrow** (verb): to dig into the earth to make a tunnel
3. **chemical composition** (noun): the combination of simple parts that make up a (homogenous) whole
4. a **chunk** (noun): a rock-like piece
5. to **connect** (verb): to think of as belonging together; to relate
6. **exquisite** (adjective): fine in detail; beautiful
7. a **glaze** (noun): a hard, shiny surface; a glossy top layer
8. **jewelry** (non-count noun): objects like necklaces, bracelets, rings
9. to **mention** (verb): to say something about
10. a **miner** (noun): a person who digs into the earth looking for valuable minerals
11. a **mineral** (noun): a metal or rock with several elements in it
12. the **native people** (plural noun): the people who have lived in an area for many generations
13. an **ore** (noun): a rock that is taken from the earth because it contains a metal or a stone that is valuable
14. to **polish** (verb): to rub to make smooth and shiny

15. **pottery** (non-count noun): containers (pots, pitchers, cups) that are made of clay

16. **precious** (adjective): valuable

17. a **prospector** (noun): a person looking for mineral wealth; a miner

18. **rubble** (non-count noun): throw-away material; material that is not useful

19. a **seam of ore** (noun): a rock layer that contains valuable minerals

20. **simultaneously** (adverb): at the same time

21. a **web** (noun): a fine, net-like trap for insects, made by a spider

22. **tailings** (plural noun): useless throw-away material from a mine, usually in a pile

23. a **tribe** (noun): a group of people; a nation (usually a small group)

24. a **vein** (noun): a blood vessel leading back to the heart; a line of ore in a seam

25. **volcanic activity** (non-count noun): occurrence of heat and ash or liquid rock coming from the earth

26. a **volcano** (noun): a mountain that can explode with heat, ash, and liquid rock

Practice the New Words

Look at the list of new words. Then read these sentences. Use the correct form of a word from the list to fill in each blank. Words in *italics* are clues to help you. There may be some words that you will use more than once and some that you will not use at all.

1. The Navajo and the Hopi are two Native American

   _____ . Among these *groups of* _____

   people, there are many talented _____ who make

   beautiful _____ like *rings and bracelets* out of

   turquoise and silver.

2. Three men went into the mountains to find gold. People like them were called _____ . They looked for gold, silver, and other kinds of _____ , such as turquoise.

3. Mount Fuji in Japan, Krakatoa in Indonesia, and Mount Vesuvius in Italy are all _____ . This *kind of mountain* is dangerous because _____ can start at any time.

4. A *piece of rock* that contains turquoise looks like any _____ of stone, except that it is blue or green. Its _____ includes both aluminum and copper.

5. To *make* a piece of turquoise *smooth and beautiful,* the jewelry maker must _____ it.

6. *Rock that contains valuable minerals* is called _____ . If it contains copper, it is probably green in color. The *people who dig into the earth* for copper, silver, or gold are _____ .

7. The teacher *told* the students about the class. He *said* that there would be homework every day. He also _____ that students would have quizzes.

8. Ceramic artists make beautiful *things out of clay.* They put a *hard and shiny* colored _____ on their _____ .

9. Gold is *very valuable.* It is a _____ metal.

10. It's not easy to laugh and cry *at the same time.* Some people cannot even walk and talk _____ .

11. Some animals _____ into the earth for safety. Some Some *dig* under trees or rocks for protection.

12. On some turquoise stone, there are many fine black or silver lines like a net. These lines _____ like the parts of a spider's _____ . These lines of silver in turquoise are also called _____ .

13. If a miner finds a thick layer of rock that has silver or gold in it, he will *dig* out the precious metal from that _____ of ore.

14. Next to many mines there are *piles* of _____ . After the miners take out the precious metal, they have

    _____ .

Find the Details

Skim and scan to find the answers to these questions.

1. What is the chemical composition of copper sulfate?

   _____

2. What are the Navajo and Hopi?   _____

3. What states are part of the American Southwest?

   _____

4. Which is the most precious metal?   _____

5. What conditions in the past resulted in turquoise stones?

   _____

6. What is a chunk of unpolished turquoise called?

   _____

7. Where can miners find turquoise today?   _____

8. How did this blue stone get the name of *Turkish*?

   _____

Give Your Opinion

Read these questions. Tell your classmates what you think.

1. Many prospectors worked very hard to "get rich quick." They left their families and went to the mountains. They worked under dangerous conditions. They dreamed of finding gold and becoming wealthy. What is your opinion about such work?

2. Would you try to get rich quick?

3. What are some modern ways of trying to get rich quick?

4. What makes something a work of art?

 Make Some Inferences

A. Circle all the right answers.

1. Which statements are probably true about prospectors?

   a. They were good farmers.

   b. They didn't own any land of their own.

   c. They dreamed of finding gold and getting rich.

   d. They were willing to work hard.

   e. Their lives were easy.

   f. They knew about gold and silver ore.

   g. They wanted to get rich quick.

2. Which statements are true about turquoise?

   a. Miners can see the blue or green color of turquoise in ore.

   b. It is found in most parts of the world.

   c. The mineral contains some copper.

   d. Turquoise is blue or green because of the aluminum in its chemical composition.

   e. The stone can be polished to a smooth surface.

   f. Turquoise is a gemstone.

   g. The brightest blue turquoise contains more copper than the greenish stones.

3. Which one in this list of statements is true about minerals in the earth?

   a. Precious metals and minerals are found together.

   b. Precious minerals are easy to find.

   c. Prospectors found large chunks of silver and gold.

   d. Gold is found with spider webs.

B. Read these questions and think about them. Then answer them.

1. Which kind of turquoise is probably most valuable—clear blue, blue with veins of silver, or dark green? Why do you think so? What makes it the most valuable? _____

2. Why do you think so many of the world's famous silversmiths (artists who work with silver and turquoise) are Navajo and Hopi? _____

3. Why is turquoise sometimes called sky stone?

   _____

 Find the Main Ideas

A. Circle the best answer.

1. What is the main idea in the second paragraph?

   a. The American Southwest has many Native American tribes.

   b. Some of the most famous turquoise artists are Native Americans.

   c. You can make belt buckles out of turquoise and silver.

   d. Texas and Nevada are part of the American Southwest.

2. Which of these titles would be a good title for the third paragraph?

   a. Gold, the Most Precious Metal

   b. The Riches in the Mountains

   c. Rubble and Tailings

   d. Turquoise from the Mines of the Southwest

3. Which title would work in place of "Sky Stones" for the whole reading?

   a. Native American Art

   b. Among the Rocks

   c. Some Facts About Turquoise

   d. Miners and Prospectors

B. Read this list of statements. One is the main idea of the whole reading. Write *MI* in the blank before that main idea. Several of the ideas are important supporting ideas. Write *SI* in the blank before each of those ideas. The rest of the ideas are details. Write *D* in the blank before each of those statements.

1. _____ The chemical composition of turquoise is aluminum phosphate, with some copper and silver in it.

2. _____ People commonly think of turquoise and silver together with Native American art.

3. _____ There are many interesting things about turquoise that most people don't know.

4. _____ Miners found turquoise in chunks of ore when they were burrowing for silver and gold.

5. _____ There is turquoise in Iran.

6. _____ Turquoise is found in Tibet.

7. _____ The name of the stone is the French word for *Turkish*.

8. _____ Colorado is in the American Southwest.

9. _____ Rubble is throw-away rock.

10. _____ Today miners dig for turquoise.

Write Your Thoughts

1. In many situations, something valuable is thrown away. What do you think about throwing away things that could be useful? Can you think of some examples?

2. Many people think that mining makes the land ugly. The piles of rubble and tailings are certainly not beautiful. What can be done about this problem for miners?

The Lost Are Found

The waters of the Mediterranean hide the lost cities of Egypt.

Prepare to Read

- Have you ever been to an ancient city?
- Have you ever seen ruins of a city? What are ruins like?
- Look at the map on the first page of this unit. What will you learn about?
- Make a list of your own new words, and try to understand the main ideas.
- Do you get any ideas from the title?

Answer These Questions

First read the story, and then try to answer these questions.

1. Where did these archeologists work?
2. Why did they read and reread some ancient Greek dramas?
3. What did this team of archeologists do that no one had ever tried before?
4. What did they find?

Read the Story

The Lost Are Found

1   Ancient Egypt was a busy place. There were many great cities, centers of business, government, and learning. Some of these cities still exist today. Many others are in ruins, but people know where these places are. However, the stories of
5   Egypt include three more great cities. And until recently there was no evidence of their location. They certainly do not exist today. Yet, even the legends of the Greeks tell of these cities. Their names were Herakleion, Canopus, and Menouthis. Where had they gone? People didn't know where
10   the cities were. Therefore, these cities were "lost." Chances are that they disappeared because of a disaster.

These lost cities were like the city of Atlantis. An important city in ancient times, Atlantis disappeared. For years scientists tried to find it. They found old stories about travelers going there. Therefore, they were able to figure out the distance to Atlantis. Today most scientists believe that Atlantis was probably on Santorini, an island in the Mediterranean. Santorini is a volcanic island. Archeologists believe that Atlantis disappeared when the volcano erupted. In the water around Santorini, there are parts of a city under the water. Most of the city is not there at all. It simply vanished. Therefore, Atlantis was a "lost" city.

What is the story about the three missing Egyptian cities? In ancient Greek dramas, there was information about them. Archeologists followed the clues in the Greek stories and continued to look for the three cities. They showed extraordinary ability because they followed the clues carefully. They looked even though there was no land where the cities were supposed to be. Archeologists started looking in Mediterranean waters! And they found all three sites. There are houses, temples, and the structures of a harbor. According to the Greeks, these cities were famous because they were very rich. These cities had huge temples; people came from distant places to see them. These people were pilgrims, making pilgrimages to holy places. They came and spent lots of money in these cities.

The three lost cities were also famous for their art. Because the temples were holy places, they were decorated with many beautiful things. Archeologists have found incredibly beautiful statues. There is a statue of the Egyptian goddess Isis that is extraordinary. It is black granite and life-size. She is wearing a beautiful long dress. Today she stands in a museum.

The city of Herakleion was a busy seaport. It was the center of shipping until Alexandria was established by
45   Alexander the Great in 331 B.C. Under the water, Herakleion appears to be whole. It seems that the whole city just sank. Nothing else changed. A French archeologist, Franck Goddio, was in charge of the team. Goddio said, "We have a complete city with temples, walls, and a harbor with 10 ancient ships."
50   One architectural structure, a stele, was found intact. It seemed to be frozen in time.

Today Herakleion lies under 20 to 30 feet of water. Goddio's team worked with modern technology to create a map of the area. They used magnetic waves to make a city plan for
55   Herakleion. In a strange way, the sea has saved the cities. Now archeologists can learn even more about the structure of cities and how the people lived. Nothing has changed since the cities sank into the water. Gaballa Ali Gaballa, the head of the Egyptian archeology, had some interesting information
60   about the cities. For example, he explained about the temples and the pilgrimages. He was able to date the cities. The Egyptians built these cities in 600 or 700 B.C.

No one knows exactly what happened to them. This area has frequent earthquakes. Perhaps it was an earthquake that
65   caused the land to fall. In any case, the sea moved over the land. The site of Herakleion is now four miles from land. It is in the Bay of Abu Qir. The best guess of the archeologists is that the disaster happened in the seventh or eighth century A.D. And now, the lost are lost no more.

Now go back to *Answer These Questions*.

Can you answer the questions? If not, then read the story again and continue the lesson. Go back to the questions at the end of the unit. Perhaps you will have answers then.

Learn the New Words

Here are some of the new words and meanings in this reading.

1. **ancient** (adjective): very old; of historical times
2. a **bay** (noun): a protected part of a larger body of water; a natural harbor
3. to **be decorated** (verb): to be made beautiful by having beautiful things added
4. a **clue** (noun): a hint; evidence to help solve a puzzle
5. to **date** (verb): to determine the time in history
6. a **disaster** (noun): a natural happening that causes great damage, such as a storm or earthquake
7. a **drama** (noun): a theater production; a play
8. to **erupt** (verb): to explode with ash or lava (as a volcano)
9. **evidence** (non-count noun): proof that something was there
10. to **exist** (verb): to be; to live
11. to **figure out** (idiom): to think about and find a solution to
12. a **harbor** (noun): a place where ships can go to land safely
13. **huge** (adjective): very large; great in size
14. **in ruins** (idiom): in a broken-down condition
15. **intact** (adjective): whole; unbroken
16. a **legend** (noun): a story that may or may not be real
17. a **location** (noun): a place
18. **magnetic waves** (plural noun): electrical impulses used to measure distance
19. a **pilgrim** (noun): a person who travels to a holy place
20. a **pilgrimage** (noun): a trip to a holy place
21. a **seaport** (noun): a harbor city; a city where ships came to land

22. a **stele** (noun): a large piece of stone with an inscription (writing) on it

23. to **vanish** (verb): to disappear; to leave without any signs of existing

Practice the New Words

A. Look at the list of new words. Then read these sentences. Use the correct form of a word from the list to fill in each blank. Words in *italics* are clues to help you. There may be some words that you will use more than once and some that you will not use at all.

1. There are many *stories* about Alexander the Great. These

   _____ may or may not be true, but they contain

   a great deal of information about the man.

2. After the earthquake, much of the city of Kobe was

   _____ .

3. According to Greek history, *many years ago* in _____

   times, a _____ statue of a man stood over the way

   into the _____ of the island of Rhodes. Ships

   came into the _____ and passed between the legs

   of the *very large* statue. The statue made the city of Rhodes a

   very famous for *sailors* on the Mediterranean Sea.

4. An earthquake is one kind of natural _____ .
   There is another kind of natural *danger* when a volcano

   _____ .

5. For people of the Muslim faith, a *visit to the holy city of Mecca*

   is an important goal. Such a _____ gives a

   person special blessings. A *person who goes to Mecca* is a

   _____ .

6. No one knows for certain exactly *where Atlantis was*. Its

   _____ has been a great mystery to scientists.
   There are so many stories, however, that they are certain that
   the city _____ , even though there is little

   _____ of where it was.

7. Scientists can use special tools, such as _____ ,
   to find lost cities under the water.

8. For many years, people near Naples told stories about the

   city of Pompeii. According to the _____ , there
   was a city under the volcanic ash. Archeologists tried to

   _____ where the ruins of Pompeii could be. They
   listened to the stories. Then they began to dig. They found the

   old city of Pompeii _____ . (Everything was as
   it was when Mount Vesuvius erupted and buried the city in
   ashes.)

9. They were like detectives, following _____ to
   figure out a mystery.

10. The scientists were able to determine how old the city was.

    They _____ it as 2,000 years old.

11. Some of the buildings _____ with beautiful
    paintings.

12. In ancient Greece, the people went to their theaters frequently.

    They enjoyed the _____ that actors put on.

B. Draw a line between the two words or phrases with similar meanings.

1. whole	a. disappear
2. vanish	b. theater production
3. map	c. huge
4. drama	d. city plan
5. story	e. be
6. very large	f. very old
7. harbor	g. clue
8. ancient	h. group of people working together
9. disaster	i. legend
10. evidence	j. volcanic eruption or earthquake
11. exist	k. intact
12. team	l. seaport

Find the Details

Skim and scan to find the answers to these questions.

1. Which three Egyptian cities were lost? _____

   _____ _____

2. What is Santorini? _____

3. Where were the three cities found? _____

4. Who is Frank Goddio? _____

5. When was Herakleion probably built? _____

6. Who is Gaballa Al Gaballa? _____

7. How old is Herakleion? _____

8. Where is the location of Herakleion now? _____

9. What probably caused the cities to vanish? _____

10. How old were the three cities when they disappeared?

    _____

Give Your Opinion

Read these questions. Tell your classmates what you think.

1. Why do people such as archeologists want to find lost cities?

2. Is what we learn from archeology important? If so, how?

3. The Egyptians are going to leave the found cities where they are. Do you think their decision is a wise one? Why or why not?

4. Some people believe it is better not to look for lost cities. Can you figure out what their reasons are? How do you feel about it?

Make Some Inferences

Circle the best answer.

1. How do we know that Herakleion, Canopus, and Menouthis were all once cities on the coast?

   a. They are under the water now.

   b. There were ships there.

   c. They have harbor structures.

   d. They are still harbor cities.

2. Archeologists usually work in groups or teams. What evidence do we have about this fact?

   a. The head of the team is a French archeologist.

   b. The information comes from the head of Egyptian archeology.

   c. The archeologists were all pilgrims.

   d. There are clues in Greek legends.

3. We know that Alexander the Great lived more than 2,000 years ago. What evidence do we have in the reading?

   a. He died in Herakleion.

   b. We know that he established the city of Alexandria in 331 B.C.

   c. His name appears in Greek dramas.

   d. He visited Atlantis on the island of Santorini.

4. What is extraordinary about the finding of the three lost cities is that…

    a. they were found so quickly.

    b. they were found where there is no land.

    c. they were found by Alexander the Great.

    d. each of them was found by a team of archeologists.

5. We know that these cities were rich because of…

    a. the beautiful buildings and their decorations.

    b. their location on the sea.

    c. the pilgrims that went there on pilgrimages.

    d. the structures of the harbors.

6. One building is surely a temple because…

    a. pilgrims who were making pilgrimages were found there.

    b. it had a beautiful statue of the ancient Egyptian goddess Isis in it.

    c. it is a structure in the harbor area of the city.

    d. today that building is a museum for the many things that archeologists found.

7. What do pilgrims do for a city?

    a. They make a lot of extra work and cause trouble.

    b. They make a need for hotels and places to visit.

    c. Pilgrims don't really do much because they don't stay long.

    d. Pilgrims make a city rich because they spend money there.

8. What is the meaning of the following sentence? *The stele was "frozen in time."*

    a. Ice and snow stopped any changes from happening to it.

    b. The stele sank into the water, and nothing changed after that.

    c. There were serious changes in the climate.

    d. Time caused great changes to occur to the stele.

Find the Main Ideas

Circle the best answer.

1. What is the work of archeologists?
   a. to study natural disasters
   b. to find evidence of history in the ruins of old cities
   c. to use modern equipment such as magnetic waves to find interesting things in the sea
   d. to study the ancient Greek dramas for evidence about history

2. What is the main idea about Atlantis?
   a. A city can vanish as a result of a natural disaster.
   b. No one knows where Atlantis was.
   c. Atlantis appears in some of the ancient Greek dramas.
   d. Archeologists are interested in lost cities.

3. What is the main idea of the reading?
   a. Natural disasters have damaged cities all over the world.
   b. Archeologists can follow clues from different sources and find lost cities.
   c. A new kind of archeology is developing from studies under water.
   d. Alexander the Great established a great ancient city.

Write Your Thoughts

1. Imagine that you are part of a team of archeologists. Which part of the world do you want to study? Why?
2. Archeology costs a lot of money. Do you think it is a good idea to spend money on such work? Why or why not?

Skippy

This harbor seal enjoys riding on a kayak.

Prepare to Read

- Throughout history, many animals have come to be friendly with people. What are some animals that we think of as tame?
- Do we need those animals? Why or why not?
- Sometimes an animal gets used to human beings and isn't afraid of people. What happens then? Is it good for the people? Is it good for the animal?
- Under what circumstances is it likely to be dangerous for the animal?
- Look at the picture on the first page of this unit. What will you learn about?
- Make a list of your own new words, and try to understand the main ideas.
- Do you get any ideas from the title? Does the name "Skippy" mean anything to you?

Answer These Questions

First read the story, and then try to answer these questions.

1. Who is Skippy?
2. Why is Skippy a problem?
3. Why is it important that a harbor seal weighs about 200 pounds (nearly 100 kilograms) as an adult?

Read the Story

Skippy

1   Every tourist who visits the Pacific Coast finds the wildlife interesting. There are hundreds of kinds of birds, for example. Some see whales as they swim north or south. Away from the shore, people frequently see dolphins.

5   In the natural bays and inlets of the Alaskan coast, there are thousands of harbor seals. They play and fish for food in the water. They are ordinary sea creatures, but they are

curious. As people go by in canoes, boats, or kayaks, the seals lift their heads from the water. From a distance of about 50 feet, they watch. They act almost like people, especially on a beach. On a sunny day, hundreds of them will climb out of the water and lie on the sand. They look friendly, but usually they keep their distance. There is now one seal that doesn't. Her name is Skippy.

Skippy was just a young pup, maybe a week old, when a man in a kayak picked her up. The baby seal was crying just like a human baby. The kayaker didn't see her mother. So he thought that her mother had abandoned her. That's why he rescued her. For four days, the baby seal rode in the kayak. She ate the camper's food—peanut butter and powdered milk.

It seems that Skippy liked that food a lot. But the food didn't like her. It made her quite sick. The biologists at the Alaska SeaLife Center in Seward took care of her. By the end of the summer, she was well again. They took her to Aialik Bay and let her go free. She weighed about 65 pounds at that time. They thought that they were saying good-bye to the happy little seal.

The next year some strange stories came back to the SeaLife Center. A harbor seal was doing some rather unusual things. This seal seemed much friendlier than other seals. The people at the SeaLife Center didn't have to wonder. They were sure it was Skippy. They checked the identification tag, and yes, it was Skippy indeed.

One of the calls came from an experienced kayaker named George Durner. He was on a kayak trip in late June. It was going to be a solo trip, but he wasn't alone long. Skippy joined him. She swam along the side of his kayak for a while. She swam around the kayak, and then she hopped onto the back of his kayak. Durner was somewhat worried. Kayaks

40   are very light and balanced to cut through the water. They can be unstable. Durner is a pro with a kayak, but not all kayakers have his experience.

     Durner works as a zoologist. He studies polar bears, but he knows about harbor seals, too. "It is not natural," he said. "On 45 the other hand, it's interesting to have a seal hang out with me." He had the opportunity to observe the seal closely. As a scientist, Durner enjoyed having a seal as a kayaking buddy.

     Wildlife biologists have some concerns. Harbor seals grow to as much as 200 pounds. If a 200-pound Skippy 50 jumped out of the water onto a kayak, the kayak could tip over. Not all visitors to the area are likely to be zoologists like George Durner. Someone might be frightened of the friendly seal and shoot it. Kaja Brix, a biologist at the National Marine Fisheries Service, shares this belief. "We don't want 55 an injury to a person or a seal," she said.

     What will happen to a seal that ate Skippy® brand peanut butter as a baby? She may not be able to live free and safely in the wild. It might be necessary for her to live in a wild animal center or a zoo. She likes people too much, and she seems to 60 have no fear.

Now go back to *Answer These Questions*.

Can you answer the questions? If not, then read the story again and continue the lesson. Go back to these questions at the end of the unit. Perhaps you will have answers then.

Learn the New Words

Here are some of the new words and meanings in this reading.

1. to **abandon** (verb): to leave unprotected
2. **balanced** (adjective): having equal weight on both sides

3. a **beach** (noun): a sandy shore of a sea, ocean, or lake

4. a **canoe** (noun): a long and narrow boat-like water craft

5. a **coast** (noun): a long line where land and sea meet

6. a **concern** (noun): a worry; something to think about as a problem to solve

7. **curious** (adjective): wanting to know more

8. a **dolphin** (noun): a sea animal that is friendly to people

9. to **hang out with** (idiom): to stay close to like a friend

10. a **harbor seal** (noun): a sea animal that lives near the shore

11. to **hop** (verb): to jump up

12. an **inlet** (noun): a small bay; a protected natural harbor

13. a. a **kayak** (noun): a one-person canoe
    b. a **kayaker** (noun): a person who uses a kayak

14. to **keep one's distance** (idiom): to stay away from; to avoid

15. an **opportunity** (noun): a time for trying something; a chance

16. a **pro** (noun): a professional who is experienced at something

17. a **pup** (noun): a baby of some kinds of animals, such as a dog or a seal

18. to **rescue** (verb): to take out of danger

19. **solo** (adjective): alone; without another person

20. to **tip over** (idiom): to capsize; to turn upside-down in the water

21. **unstable** (adjective): out of balance; easily upset

22. a **whale** (noun): the largest animal in the world, a sea mammal

23. **wildlife** (non-count noun) all wild animals and plants together

23. to **wonder** (verb): to think about; to question

25. a **zoologist** (noun): a biologist; an animal scientist

Practice the New Words

A. Look at the list of new words. Then read these sentences. Use the correct form of a word from the list to fill in each blank. There may be some words that you will use more than once and some that you will not use at all.

1. A _____ is likely to know about wild animals like whales, dolphin, harbor seals, and polar bears.

2. If a boat is unstable, it is easy for it to _____ .

3. Along the road, you can sometimes see broken-down cars. Their owners _____ them because they do not want to pay for repairs.

4. That man plays the piano so well that he must be a

   _____ .

5. The largest animal in the world is a sea animal, a _____

6. A trip that a person takes alone is a _____ trip.

7. If you are concerned about a situation, you will

   _____ until you know it is safe.

8. A kayak is a carefully _____ kind of canoe. It can _____ easily. In fact, a kayak can seem rather _____ to an inexperienced kayaker.

9. Bears and wolves are two dangerous kinds of

   _____ .

10. If you ever have an _____ , visit Iceland!

11. The harbor seals were playing on the _____ in the small _____ . The photographers with their cameras were out in a boat on the bay.

12. Which kind of boat is easier to handle—a _____ or a _____ ?

13. She has a _____ about the cost of an education.

    She is _____ how much it will cost.

14. At the zoo we saw lots of babies, such as seal baby bears and
    seal _____ .

15. The wind made the water dangerous, and one kayaker

    _____ ,but a friend was there to help. He

    _____ the kayaker.

16. Some animals want to know what's happening. They are

    _____ animals.

17. There is a road along the sea. It goes up and down the

    _____ .

B. Draw a line between the two words or phrases with similar
meanings.

1. canoe	a. harbor seal
2. zoologist	b. unstable
3. dolphin	c. chance
4. bay	d. alone
5. help	e. kayak
6. opportunity	f. beach
7. concern	g. inlet
8. not balanced	h. rescue
9. solo	i. worry
10. coast	j. biologist

Find the Details

Skim and scan to answer these questions.

1. Where does Skippy live? _____

2. How old was Skippy when she was picked up by a kayaker?

   _____

3. Why did the kayaker pick her up? _____

4. What did the kayaker feed the baby seal? _____

5. What made Skippy sick? _____

6. What is the Alaska SeaLife Center? _____

7. What is Aialik Bay? Why is it important in this story?

   _____

8. How did the people at the Alaska SeaLife Center know that the

   friendly seal was Skippy? _____

9. Who is Kaja Brix? _____

10. Why are kayaks unstable? _____

 Give Your Opinion

Read these questions. Tell your classmates what you think.

1. It was probably fortunate for Skippy that George Durner "met" her before other kayakers. Can you explain why?

2. Is it a good idea for wild animals to be tamed? Why or why not?

3. What would you do about the Skippy problem if you were a worker at the Alaska SeaLife Center?

4. Zoologists know about a phenomenon called "imprinting." They know, for example, that a baby duck will follow a human being who is there when the duck hatches. (Usually, a baby duck first sees its own mother.) Because of imprinting, some animals seem to think that a human being is its mother. Do you think that's what happened to Skippy?

5. The biologists at the National Marine Fisheries Service see Skippy as a problem and a danger. Do you agree or disagree with them?

Make Some Inferences

Read and think about these questions. Then try to answer them.

1. How did Skippy get her name? _____

2. George Durner works with polar bears, but he also knows about seals. Why should he be an expert on seals, too?

   _____

3. What made Skippy sick when she was a baby? Why did she get sick from it? _____

4. What do seals usually eat? _____

5. Why is it not surprising that a zoologist in Alaska is a pro with a kayak? _____

6. George Durner went out on a kayak trip alone. However, his trip was not a solo trip. Why not? _____

7. Skippy is a seal, but she is also harbor seal. What can you infer from that information? _____

8. What is the purpose of fear? _____

9. Why will Skippy probably have to live in a zoo?

   _____

10. Why might a person shoot Skippy? _____

11. Why is Skippy more dangerous to kayakers as an adult than as a young seal? _____

12. Why do harbor seals lift their heads out of the water to watch kayakers go by? _____

Find the Main Ideas

A. Write a check (✓) next to each true statement.

1. _____ Skippy is a whale.

2. _____ Baby seals are called pups.

3. _____ A seal pup cries like a human baby.

4. _____ Seals live in the ocean along the Alaska coast.

5. _____ Seals like to play on a beach, just like people.

6. _____ Campers often carry peanut butter and powdered milk because it is good food for seals.

7. _____ Aialik Bay is home to many harbor seals.

8. _____ The Alaska SeaLife Center is in Canada.

9. _____ An adult harbor seal weighs almost 100 kilograms.

10. _____ Some Alaskan seals have identification tags on them.

11. _____ There are no polar bears in Alaska.

12. _____ Sea kayaking is a popular sport.

13. _____ Most people enjoy seeing the wildlife of Alaska.

14. _____ There are whales in the same places as seals along the coast of Alaska.

15. _____ A wild animal that likes people is probably not safe in the wild.

B. Circle the best answer.

1. What is the main idea about the Alaska SeaLife Center?

   a. Seals can become very friendly animals.

   b. The SeaLife Center is there to protect people and animals.

   c. Biologists do polar bear research there.

   d. It is a zoo where people can see all kinds of Alaskan wildlife.

2. What is the main idea about the relationship between wild animals and people?

   a. All animals should keep their distance from people.

   b. The natural relationship between animals and people is fear.

   c. People should keep their distance from wild animals.

   d. People should always help wild animals.

3. Choose the best one of these titles for the story.

   a. A Seal Who Likes People

   b. George Durner and the Harbor Seal

   c. Alaskan Wildlife

   d. Adventures of a Kayaker

Write Your Thoughts

1. If you see a wild baby animal, what do you think you should do? Should you rescue a baby bird? What could you do to protect it?

2. Find the name and address of a wildlife center or zoo. Write a letter to ask for information about wild animals in your area.

3. George Durner says about Skippy, "It's not natural. On the other hand, it's interesting to have a seal hang out with me." What do you think he found interesting? Why did he watch Skippy closely? What do you think he probably learned about harbor seals?

Fight Fire with Fire

Oregon hot shot Ron Schmitt

Prepare to Read

Which of these words and ideas will you probably see in this unit? Circle them.

fire	airplanes
tools	equipment
danger	harbor seals
boats	sports
lightning	satellite communication
water	chemical information
weather information	

- What other ideas do you get from the title of this unit?
- Look at the picture on the first page of this unit. What will you learn about?
- Make a list of your own new words, and try to understand the main ideas.

Answer These Questions

First read the story, and then try to answer these questions.

1. Why has firefighting become a science?
2. Why is it difficult to fight fires on mountains?
3. What causes most fires?
4. Who puts out fires?

Read the Story

Fight Fire with Fire

1   The forest fire was moving fast up the side of a mountain. There were many homes up there on the slopes, for people and animals. The firefighters were exhausted. They had expected other firefighters, a fresh new team. However, they were called

5　to another fire. A new strategy was in order. The experts met, and they talked. What could they do to stop the fire before it destroyed everything on the mountain? This time, the decision was to fight fire with fire. They called the helicopters.

10　Helicopters came in with plastic fire balls. They dropped the fire balls in specific places. Inside each ball was a mixture of chemicals that would explode into flames on impact. It starts to burn as soon as it hits ground. Because of the direction of the wind, the experts knew the old fire and the new fire would meet. It would help them control the burning.
15　Another advantage is safety. Fighting a fire on a mountain is dangerous work. Fighting any fire is dangerous, but steep slopes and rocks make it more difficult.

Battling the orange monster (fire) has become a modern science. Experts have developed many new techniques.
20　Fighting fire with fire is just one of them. In the long dry summer, lightning causes hundreds of fires on open land. The dry grass and leaves of "wildlands" ignite rapidly, and fire can spread very fast. Ways of finding fires and stopping them from spreading, therefore, are very important. Great
25　forest areas have fire towers. Watchers search for signs of smoke. Where there is smoke, there is fire. Nowadays, the Global Positioning System can locate a fire precisely, using satellite communications. Airplanes with heat-sensing equipment can find a fire fast too, sometimes even before
30　there is much smoke. Sometimes there is a lot of dry lightning (lightning without rain). Heat-sensing aircraft go up to find hot spots. Prevention of fire spread is important in firefighting.

Climate experts are also firefighters. A meteorologist is a weather and climate expert. One kind of meteorologist works
35　on microclimates; that is, the expert determines what the conditions are in a very small area. Are the winds going up

or down, north or south? According to the conditions, one technique or another will work best. Thus a fire meteorologist is a member of a fire team.

40   Most of the firefighting work depends on people. Men and women work with shovels, hoses, chain saws, bulldozers, and axes. Their job is to stop the progress of a fire. They attempt to hold back the fire by making a non-burn zone. They call this area a "fuel break." If there is nothing to burn,

45   the fire will stop. So they dig ditches, and they clear away dry grass and brush. They use chain saws and axes to clear a path. They hope the fire will not cross over the fuel break. If the burning trees are tall and there is a wind, there is danger of a crown fire. In a crown fire, the flames jump from tree top

50   to tree top and burn from top to bottom.

Helicopter and airplane pilots are also part of every fire team. Special aircraft can carry water or flame-retardant. Water extinguishes flames, and it is cheap. A huge tanker aircraft with one pilot flies over the fires and drops water on the fire.

55   They also drop flame-retardant. This chemical mixture is thick and sticky. It is also colored red, so pilots can see it from the air. It sticks to the trees and cools them. Then they are less likely to catch on fire. Some helicopters can fight fires with lake water. They hover over a lake, drop a hose

60   into the water, and pump water into their tanks. Then they fly off to drop the water on burning trees. And back they go to the lake for more water.

These two kinds of aircraft can be dangerous to each other. That's why airplanes work on one side of a fire and

65   helicopters on the other. They never work close together.

Cleanup after a fire is also important. Firefighters with shovels look for hot spots that could burn again. Heat-sensing aircraft fly over, and crews check on equipment There are

70   many with fire extinguishers on their backs. They look for
small fires that might grow fast if the wind starts to blow.
Controlling fires in the long, hot summer is hot, hard work.

Now go back to *Answer These Questions.*

Can you answer the questions? If not, then read the story again and
continue the lesson. Go back to the questions at the end of the unit.
Perhaps you will have answers then.

Learn the New Words

Here are some of the new words and meanings in this reading.

1. (an) **aircraft** (count or non-count noun): airplanes and helicopters
   in general; an example is an airplane or a helicopter
2. an **ax** (noun): a sharp-edged tool for cutting wood, used to cut
   down trees
3. to **be in order** (verb): to be organized as it should be
4. a **bulldozer** (noun): a large, earth-moving machine used in digging
   big holes and clearing land
5. a **chain saw** (noun): a saw with a motor on it, used to cut down
   trees
6. a **crown fire** (idiom): a forest fire that spreads through the tops
   of trees, not at ground level
7. a **ditch** (noun): a long, human-made hole, through which water
   can flow
8. to **explode** (verb): to burst into fire; to go off; to blow up
9. to **extinguish** (verb): to put out; to stop
10. a **flame** (noun): a red-yellow light of a small fire (such as a match)
11. a **flame-retardant** (noun): a chemical substance that reduces
    burning ability
12. a **fuel break** (noun): an area that has been cleared of burnable
    materials to stop a fire

13. a **helicopter** (noun): a vehicle that flies; an aircraft with a turning top blade

14. a **hose** (noun): a long, flexible tube for moving water from one place to another

15. to **hover** (verb): to float in the air above one place

16. to **ignite** (verb): to start a fire with a spark

17. a **microclimate** (noun): the general weather conditions in a small area (affected by mountains, forest growth, bodies of water, and things like that)

18. **precisely** (adverb): exactly

19. a **slope** (noun): an incline

20. **steep** (adjective): said of a hill that rises quickly

21. a **strategy** (noun): a plan for solving a problem

22. a **tanker** (noun): a large vehicle (truck, aircraft, or ship) for carrying liquid

23. **wildlands** (plural noun): open or forest areas where wild animals live

Practice the New Words

Look at the list of new words. Then read these sentences. Use the correct form of a word from the list to fill in each blank. Words in *italics* are clues to help you. There may be some words that you will use more than once and some that you will not use at all.

1. Many people have summer homes on the *sides of mountains*. There are _____ roads that go up the _____ of the hills. Those people need strong vehicles to climb those hills.

2. In the summer, lightning *starts* many forest *fires*. The electricity _____ the dry grass and dry leaves.

3. Two *kinds of* _____ are the *airplane* and the _____ . The advantage to the second kind is that it can _____ in the air *above one spot*.

4. A firefighting helicopter is probably also a _____ .
   It can drop a _____ into a lake, pull many gallons
   of water into its *tanks*, and then fly to a fire and drop the water.

5. In order to fight fire with fire, a weather expert will figure out the
   weather conditions of the _____ in the area of the
   fire. Next the team will decide which *plans* or _____
   they will use to stop the fire.

6. Some of the most common firefighting *tools* are shovels, water
   hoses, _____ , _____ , and
   _____ .

7. A fire that spreads from *tree top* to tree top is a _____

8. A match produces a single *bit of fire*. It is called a
   _____ .

9. Water and _____ are dropped from tankers to
   _____ a fire. Water *puts out* a fire quickly.

10. Firefighters use a great deal of heavy equipment like bulldozers
    and simple tools like shovels to dig long deep _____
    and also to make _____ to stop a fire from spreading.
    (If there is nothing to burn, the fire stops.)

11. A Global Positioning System can locate _____
    where a fire is. It helps to know *exactly* where to go.

12. After a fire, a team of firefighters checks its equipment to make
    sure that everything _____ .

Find the Details

Skim and scan to find the answers to these questions.

1. What is a slope? _____

2. How can information about a microclimate help fight a fire?

   _____

3. What three things do helicopter pilots drop in the area of a fire?

   _____ _____ _____

4. What work does heat-sensing equipment do? _____

5. What is the value of fire towers? _____

6. What is a hot spot? _____

7. How do satellites help fight fires? _____

8. Why is wind direction important to firefighters?

   _____

9. What tools do firefighters use to cut down trees?

   _____

10. What is a flame-retardant like? _____

Figure Out the Sequence

What happens first? In the blank in front of each sentence, write a number between 1 and 10 to show what happens next.

a. _____   Aircraft with heat-sensing equipment locate the center of the fire.

b. _____   The firefighters learn about the fire and begin to organize to fight it.

c. _____   People and equipment move to the area of the fire.

d. _____   The firefighters and the vehicles with equipment clean up and leave the area.

e. _____ The Global Positioning System sees that a forest fire is starting.

f. _____ Experts decide which strategies to use.

g. _____ The fire is put out.

h. _____ The Global Positioning System tells the firefighting office about the fire.

i. _____ Lightning or careless people start a forest fire.

j. _____ Firefighters follow the strategies to stop the fire.

Give Your Opinion

Read these questions. Tell your classmates what you think.

1. In some places, people in prisons work in teams to help fight fires. Do you think it is right to ask prisoners to do such work?

2. Firefighters cut down some trees in fighting a fire. What do you think of this idea?

3. Sometimes firefighters start a second fire to fight a bigger fire. Why do you think they do it? Isn't it a mistake to start more fires?

4. Firefighters call a forest fire an orange monster. What is your opinion of this name?

Make Some Inferences

Circle all the right answers.

1. Firefighters work in teams because...
   a. one person can't do much to stop a fire.
   b. one person working alone against a fire is in greater danger because he or she doesn't know the whole picture.
   c. one team will try to do a better job than another team.
   d. people who work together often can do a job faster and better than people who do not know one another.
   e. a team of people knows how to describe a situation to others clearly.

f. some firefighting jobs require more than one person.

g. they are afraid to work alone.

2. A Global Positioning System must be able to...

a. put out a small fire immediately.

b. locate a fire precisely.

c. tell firefighters exactly where a fire is.

d. use a satellite system.

e. send aircraft to get water.

f. understand the microclimate.

g. help meteorologists determine the microclimate.

3. A pilot in a firefighting aircraft always flies alone. Which of these ideas is probably the reason for it?

a. A firefighting pilot must pay attention to the job and not to other people.

b. The job is too dangerous to risk two people.

c. Only one person can fly such an aircraft.

d. There is only one seat in that kind of aircraft.

4. Airplanes and helicopters never fight fires in the same small area. Which of the sentences below show the reasons for keeping them separate?

a. A pilot cannot watch for other aircraft and fight the fire at the same time.

b. Helicopters can rise and hit airplanes.

c. Airplanes and helicopters use different systems to fly.

d. Airplane pilots don't like helicopter pilots.

e. The microclimate might not be good for one or the other kind of aircraft.

Find the Main Idea

Which of these ideas is the main idea of the reading? Write *MI* in the blank in front of that idea. Which ideas are support ideas? Write *SI* in the blank in front of each of those ideas.

1. _____ Cleanup after a fire is an important part of the job.

2. _____ Airplanes and helicopters can fight fires, but not in the same place.

3. _____ There are fire towers and fire watchers in great forest areas.

4. _____ The fighting of forest fires has become a modern science.

5. _____ Sometimes you have to use fire to fight a fire.

6. _____ A microclimate expert can help fight a fire.

7. _____ There are teams of people who work together to fight fires.

Write Your Thoughts

1. Make a list of all the ways in the reading to stop a fire. Then organize the ideas so that you can write a paragraph about these methods.

2. Firefighting has become a science. What sciences are parts of fighting fires?

3. Imagine the work of a firefighter. How is it dangerous?

9 Another One Exactly Like the First

DNA holds all the information to create life.

Twins are a natural kind of clone. Two babies who are almost exactly alike are identical twins.

Prepare to Read

- When are two animals exactly alike?
- What is DNA? Why is it important?
- Look at the pictures on the first page of this unit. What will you learn about?
- Make a list of your own new words, and try to understand the main ideas.
- Do you get any ideas from the title?

Answer These Questions

First read the story, and then try to answer these questions.

1. Why does an animal have characteristics like hair color or size?
2. Why are scientists interested in working to change DNA?
3. What concerns are there about DNA research?
4. How can research in DNA help people? What answers to serious problems are possible in DNA research?

Read the Story

Another One Exactly Like the First

1   What do you know about eggs? Do you know how they work to make babies? You probably know that baby chicks hatch from eggs. You probably know that every animal has a mother and father. Mother chickens (hens) lay the eggs.
5   Father chickens are roosters. Most of the egg comes from the hen, but a tiny part comes from the rooster. The rooster's part combines with part of the hen's egg to form a fertilized nucleus. The nucleus is just a very small part of an egg. The rest of the egg is mostly food. It feeds the fertilized nucleus.
10   The fertilized nucleus contains all the "information" needed for the egg to become a chicken. The chick gets some of its mother's characteristics and some from its father. The part of

the nucleus with the information for those characteristics is the
DNA. In fact, DNA is like a plan for a living thing, a blueprint.

15　　　Among human beings, a baby usually resembles one
parent or the other. Identical twins, who come from the same
egg, begin life exactly alike. Most children have characteristics
of each parent. The DNA makes sure that it happens. It works
that way with other animals, too.

20　　　Biologists have done a lot of work with fertilized eggs of
chickens and other animals. They know how to take the
fertilized nucleus out of an egg. It takes a lot of skill. They
have to work very carefully. They can also replace one
nucleus with another nucleus. Then the new nucleus will
25　　grow in the egg into a different chicken. Sometimes the
biologists substitute the nucleus with one from a different
kind of bird, like a duck. The DNA from a duck replaces the
DNA of the chicken. That egg will not become a chicken. It
will grow into a different kind of bird, a duck.

30　　　Biologists have done the same kind of experiment with
mammals as well as birds. Scientists have also done other
experiments with the DNA from different creatures. The
results have been some very surprising animals. For example,
jellyfish are naturally fluorescent; they make light when they
35　　swim. In Japan, the light-making DNA from jellyfish was
added to the DNA of mice. The new mice glow in the dark.

In Scotland, DNA from human beings was used to make
a new drug. Some biologists added human DNA to the DNA
of sheep. The new sheep produce a drug to treat cystic fibrosis.
40　　Cystic fibrosis is a terrible disease. A person's lungs become
filled with fibers. Then the person can't breathe. The new drug
helps a person with this disease breathe easier and live longer.

There are some other interesting possibilities. One concerns woolly mammoths. These mammals lived 20,000 years ago. They were huge, nine-ton creatures. They looked kind of like elephants. They lived at the same time and same places as human beings. Some of the mammoths lived in Siberia. At that time Siberia was much warmer than it is now. Grass and trees grew there. But suddenly the climate changed. It got very, very cold! The cold froze some mammoths in mud. It was like a big deep freeze. The mammoths' flesh became frozen hard. It stayed frozen for 20,000 years. Some of the cells in the frozen flesh have DNA in good shape. This DNA can replace the DNA in an elephant's egg. The egg with the new DNA could be put into another elephant. If all of the theory is right, the egg with the mammoth DNA will grow into a baby mammoth. Then the mammoth will no longer be extinct.

Experiments with animals are teaching scientists a great deal about DNA. There are already clones, animals that are exactly like other animals. These animals are the result of genetic experiments. In a sense, they don't have parents. They result from making the DNA of one animal copy itself into another animal. Through such work, biologists may be able to help improve all animal life. For example, they might be able to choose characteristics. They could make sheep with longer wool. Or perhaps they would make smarter dogs. Another aspect is that they might be able to destroy weaknesses to disease. Making another one just like the first is an extraordinary kind of science.

Now go back to *Answer These Questions.*

Can you answer the questions? If not, then read the story again and continue the lesson. Go back to the questions at the end of the unit. Perhaps you will have answers then.

 ## Learn the New Words

Here are some of the new words and meanings in this reading.

1. to **be extinct** (verb): to not exist because the last of the species has died

2. a **characteristic** (noun): a personal feature; a way of telling two things apart; a single distinguishing aspect of one thing compared to another (such as color of hair for a person, or kind of flower or leaf for a plant)

3. a **clone** (noun): a copy; an animal or plant made from the DNA of another animal or plant

4. a **creature** (noun): an animal; a living being

5. **cystic fibrosis** (non-count noun): a disease that fills the lungs with fiber-like growths

6. **fertilized** (adjective): able to grow; helped to grow

7. **flesh** (non-count noun): meat and muscles; body that is not bone

8. **fluorescent** (adjective): said of things that give off light

9. a. to **freeze** (verb): to become hard like ice from the cold (past tense = *froze*)

   b. **frozen** (adjective): hard like ice from the cold

10. **genetic** (adjective): related to DNA research

11. to **hatch** (verb): to come out of an egg and begin to live as a baby (said of birds)

12. a **mammoth** (noun): a huge, elephant-like animal that has been extinct for 20,000 years

13. a **mouse** (noun): a small rodent; an animal used in experiments (plural = *mice*)

14. a **nucleus** (noun): the center of a cell

15. to **replace** (verb): to put a different thing in the place of another; to substitute

16. to **resemble** (verb): to look like

17. a **skill** (noun): a special ability; a talent

18. to **substitute** (verb): to remove one thing and put a different one in its place

19. **woolly** (adjective): having lots of long hair (said of sheep and other animals)

Practice the New Words

A. Look at the list of new words. Then read these sentences. Use the correct form of a word from the list to fill in each blank. Words in *italics* are clues to help you. There may be some words that you will use more than once and some that you will not use at all.

1. Chickens, ducks, and other birds all _____ from *eggs*.

2. An egg needs to be _____ by a father before it will grow into a baby bird.

3. Every animal has some _____ of each of its parents.

4. Two identical twins begin life with the same _____ information, or *DNA*.

5. An animal that comes from the DNA of another animal is called a _____ .

6. _____ is the name of a lung disease.

7. Today we still have *elephants*, but the _____ no
   no longer exists. This *animal* is _____ . This
   huge _____ *looked like* an elephant, but it also
   _____ a *sheep* because it had _____
   skin.

8. Someone found the _____ *bodies* of several
   of these extinct creatures in the *cold solid mud* of Siberia.
   The _____ of these animals included cells in
   good condition.

9. Some fish *create their own light*. These fish are

   _____ .

10. In DNA research, scientists try to *replace* some of the DNA in
    a cell nucleus with DNA from another animal. They want to
    _____ new characteristics for the old ones.

11. Scientists use *small animals for research*. For example, they
    use _____ .

12. Doing genetic research takes a lot of _____ .
    Not every scientist has this *special ability*.

B. Draw a line between the two words or phrases with similar meanings.

1. resemble	a. feature
2. frozen	b. flesh
3. animal	c. DNA
4. clone	d. woolly
5. replace	e. twin
6. genetic	f. substitute
7. skill	g. look like
8. characteristic	h. icy cold
9. long-haired	i. ability or talent
10. meat and muscle	j. creature

Find the Details

Skim and scan to find the answers to these questions.

1. What is a fertilized egg? _____

2. What information is in DNA? _____

3. How did scientists make a drug to treat cystic fibrosis?

   _____

4. What causes a person with cystic fibrosis to die?

   _____

5. When did woolly mammoths live on Earth? _____

6. How did it happen that mammoths froze in Siberia?

   _____

7. How much did a mammoth weigh? _____

8. What is a clone? _____

9. What animal might help scientists grow a new mammoth?

   _____

10. How is a clone different from an identical twin? _____

Make Some Inferences

A. Read and think about these questions. Then try to answer them.

1. Some people think that genetic research is wrong. Can you figure out some reasons for these feelings?

2. One parent has red hair, and the other parent has brown hair. What color is their child likely to have? (Think about which is more common.)

3. If Japanese scientists made a mouse that give off light in the dark, what do we know about DNA experiments between jellyfish and mice?

4. Do you think a chicken egg could grow a new mammoth? Why or why not?

B. Circle the best answer.

1. A chicken egg with DNA from a duck will always form into a...
   a. mammoth.
   b. mouse.
   c. duck.
   d. chicken.

2. Most of the chicken egg is...
   a. shell.
   b. from the father.
   c. food for the fertilized nucleus.
   d. genetic information for the baby chicken.

3. Mice that glow in the dark...
   a. like to swim.
   b. have jellyfish DNA in them.
   c. can make drugs to treat diseases in human beings.
   d. look a lot like elephants.

4. Frozen mammoth flesh contains DNA that...

   a. could make a new mammoth.

   b. glows in the dark.

   c. is just like today's elephant.

   d. could make an elephant.

5. Human DNA...

   a. does not grow well in human beings.

   b. was added to sheep DNA to make a drug to treat a human disease.

   c. has the information for glowing in the dark.

   d. is similar to the DNA of the fertilized nucleus of a chicken's egg.

Give Your Opinion

Read these questions. Tell your classmates what you think.

1. What is your opinion about genetic research?

2. What dangers do you see in DNA research?

3. Is the possibility of new medicines a good reason for DNA research?

Make Some Inferences

Read and think about these questions. Then try to answer them.

1. What happens when someone makes a mistake in genetic research?

2. Is new life that comes from genetic research special in some way?

Find the Main Ideas

Circle the best answer.

1. What is the main idea of the first paragraph?

   a. that chickens come from eggs

   b. that most of the egg of a chicken comes from the mother chicken, the hen

    c. that the nucleus of a chicken egg feeds the baby chicken

    d. that a chicken gets genetic information from both its mother and its father

2. The main idea about the genetic experiments is that…

    a. scientists can replace some characteristics of animals.

    b. chickens and ducks are really very much alike.

    c. mammals and fish have the same kinds of DNA.

    d. it is possible to make mice that glow in the dark.

3. The main idea of the paragraph about mammoths is that…

    a. mammoths are extinct.

    b. DNA from frozen mammoth cells is still alive.

    c. elephants resemble mammoths.

    d. a deep freeze kills many animals.

4. Which title is the best one for the reading?

    a. New Woolly Mammoths

    b. The Possibilities and Problems of DNA Research

    c. Clones

    d. Medical Research and DNA

Think About This Question

Here is a dilemma (a problem that is very difficult to find a solution to). What do you think about it? It may be possible for scientists to make a new human being out of the DNA from the cell of a human being. If a person gets sick and needs to have a new body part (for example, if a person's heart is diseased), should scientists grow a new person from the DNA and remove the heart from the clone to put it into the sick person? Or is the clone a person with human rights?

Write Your Thoughts

1. Write your thoughts about the dilemma about the rights of a clone.

2. A great deal of research on plants has resulted in food with certain characteristics. However, many people worry about eating these foods because they are not natural. What do you think about them? What are your concerns?

3. DNA research can help many people (such as people with cystic fibrosis), but it also causes many other worries. What laws do we need to make sure that genetic research is good for people?

Two Years in a Tree

Julia Hill spent two years living in a redwood tree to protect the tree from lumber companies. Someone attacked the tree after she left its branches. No one knows whether that tree can survive.

Prepare to Read

- Have you ever climbed a tree? What did it feel like?
- How do you feel in high places?
- How high is an 18-story building?
- Look at all the pages in this unit. What will you learn about?
- Make a list of your own new words, and try to understand the main ideas.
- Do you get any ideas from the title?

Answer These Questions

First read the story, and then try to answer these questions.

1. Why did Julia Hill climb a redwood tree?
2. Why did she need friends to help her?
3. How did she tell her story to the world?
4. Why did she want to tell her story?

Read the Story

Two Years in a Tree

1   On December 10, 1997, Julia Hill climbed a tree. She must have liked it there. She stayed for two years! She climbed 55 meters up into the branches of a California redwood. That is as high as an 18-story building. Julia Hill wanted to protect
5   a tree. She named the tree *Luna*, or *Moon*. This tree, and many other redwoods, is on private land. The owner of the land, the Pacific Lumber Company, planned to cut down these ancient trees. Julia wanted to stop them. She could stop the destruction of Luna and an old-growth stand of old
10   redwoods. No one would cut down a tree with a person in it. So up she climbed. She was 23 years old at that time.

Julia Hill is an environmentalist. She loves all things in nature. She was particularly sad about those redwoods. They are among the largest trees on Earth. They are very old. These

15 trees were old growth. That means no one had ever cut the trees there. Redwoods are magnificent. They commonly grow to 275 feet (84 meters). They grow only in northern California, near the coast. They grow well in the foggy climate there. Many redwoods are protected in national parks. However, the

20 tree that Julia wanted to protect was not.

In her tree, Julia got a lot of attention. People wanted to know why she was there. Famous people came to visit her. They talked to her to understand her reasons. They told other people. Then reporters brought television cameras to

25 interview her.

"My feet will not touch the ground," she said, "until there is a signature on paper saying that they've protected the area." In other words, Julia and her friends hoped to save these redwoods.

30 From her tree, Julia could see the ocean. She could also see where a mudslide had destroyed seven homes in the town of Stafford. Environmentalists believe that the cutting of the trees is the reason for the mudslides. The roots of trees hold the soil in place. Without the trees, the soil can slide off the

35 hills. Mudslides cause a great deal of damage. Unfortunately, they are common in California.

Julia was an advertisement for the environment. Her actions helped many people understand the importance of these trees to the environment.

40 Julia lived a simple life in Luna. Her house was just a flat piece of wood, about two meters square. Everything she did happened right there on that piece of wood. She was cold through two winters. The fog and mists would pass through

all the clothes, even three pairs of pants and three coats! In
45 her tree home, Julia heated water on a little stove for sponge
baths. She slept under a heavy tarp. It was her protection
from the rain.

She used a bucket for a toilet. She cooked simple food
like vegetables and rice. She listened to her radio and
50 answered about 300 letters a week. She wrote a book about
Luna too. She also talked to people on her cell phone. Her
friends brought her water, food, batteries for the radio and
phone, and letter paper. They took her letters to the post
office for her. She kept in touch with the outside world. She
55 told her own story.

Julia had to work hard to stay healthy. She exercised
regularly. For example, she climbed around in the tree. She
also did sit-ups and push-ups. But it was not easy to stay fit.
She missed Mother Earth. She said, "I can't imagine how
60 incredible it's going to feel just to be able to touch the solid
earth again."

Many people disagreed with Julia and her friends. They
believe that cutting trees is good. A forest will grow again.
Julia is, they say, an eco-terrorist; she is a person who is
65 using a threat to win a battle. In any case, talks between the
lumber company and the environmentalists continued. Julia
Hill and her supporters agreed to pay $50,000 to the company.
That money was to make up for the money the company
lost. The company gave the money to a local university for
70 the study of forests. In return, Luna and the trees within 200
feet are safe.

On December 18, 1999, Pacific Lumber signed the agreement. Luna was safe at last. Then Julia Hill came down from the tree. Her arms were strong as she climbed down.

75 Her feet touched the earth. She felt solid earth under her feet. She smiled at the reporters. However, Julia had a problem. She had difficulty walking. She was 25 years old. She had not walked in two years.

Now go back to *Answer These Questions.*

Can you answer the questions? If not, then read the story again and continue the lesson. Go back to the questions at the end of the unit. Perhaps you will have answers then.

Learn the New Words

Here are some of the new words and meanings in this reading.

1. an **agreement** (noun): a formal contract; a legal paper
2. **ancient** (adjective): very old
3. a **battery** (noun): a small, tube-shaped object that is used to light a flashlight or play a radio; a small, chemical source of electricity
4. a **battle** (noun): a fight for a cause
5. a **cell phone** (noun): a wireless telephone (satellite communication)
6. the **climate** (non-count noun): the pattern of weather
7. a **coast** (noun): the place where land and ocean meet
8. to **disagree** (verb): to have a different opinion
9. an **eco-terrorist** (noun): an environmentalist who uses a threat to win
10. **fit** (adjective): healthy
11. **foggy** (adjective): covered in a cloud-like substance close to the earth
12. to **interview** (verb): to ask a person questions about a topic

13. a **mist** (noun): a light, foggy rain

14. a **mudslide** (noun): a natural disaster in which a layer of earth gets very wet from rain and goes down a hill, often taking structures and plants with it

15. **nature** (non-count noun): the untouched environment; plants and animals

16. **old-growth** (adjective): never cut; original

17. a **push-up** (noun): an exercise in which a person lies down, facing the floor, and then puts his or her hands flat on the floor and pushes himself or herself up on the toes

18. a **signature** (noun): a legal signing of one's name (to a contract or letter)

19. a **sit-up** (noun): an exercise in which a person lies on his or her back and then sits up, with the legs staying on the floor

20. to **slide** (verb): to go smoothly along a slippery surface; to slip

21. a **sponge bath** (noun): a bath in which one washes with water in a bucket and a cloth or sponge dipped into the water

22. **square** (adjective): equal in length and width

23. a **stand of trees** (idiom): a group of uncut trees

24. a **tarp** (noun): a thick, waterproof cover of heavy cloth

Practice the New Words

A. Look at the list of new words. Choose the best answer for each question or the phrase to complete the sentence.

1. What did Julia's friends bring her for the radio and phone?

   a. letters   c. food

   b. paper   d. batteries

2. How did Julia stay fit?

   a. She went for long walks in the forest.

   b. She climbed around in the tree.

   c. She swam in the ocean.

   d. She listened to the radio.

3. Julia didn't have a regular telephone to talk to friends, but she had a…

   a. radio.

   b. cell phone.

   c. small stove.

   d. good tarp.

4. The _____ of the California coast is foggy and rainy.

   a. nature

   b. mist

   c. stand

   d. climate

5. An environmentalist who acts to stop damage from people may be called…

   a. an environment.

   b. an old-growth stand.

   c. an eco-terrorist.

   d. a tarp.

6. Many people believe that trees' roots can prevent a _____ on a wet hill.

   a. push-up

   b. mist

   c. sit-up

   d. mudslide

7. Exercise is necessary to stay…

   a. push-up.

   b. fit.

   c. foggy.

   d. health.

8. If a table is 1 meter long and 1 meter wide, then it is…

   a. square.

   b. fit.

   c. old-growth.

   d. natural.

B. Find the word or phrase in the column on the right that means almost the same as the word in the column on the left. Write the letter in the blank.

1. _____ old-growth   a. healthy
2. _____ sit-up   b. mist
3. _____ fit   c. fight to win a goal
4. _____ environment   d. type of exercise
5. _____ fog   e. formal legal paper
6. _____ agreement   f. natural surroundings
7. _____ interview   g. have different ideas
8. _____ disagree   h. ancient
9. _____ battle   i. line between land and water
10. _____ coast   j. ask questions and record
                              answers

Find the Details

Skim and scan to find the answers to these questions.

1. When did Julia come down from the tree? _____

2. Who owned the land and the tree? _____

3. What was the name of the lumber company? _____

4. What is Julia's last name? _____

5. How old was Julia when she came down from the tree?

   _____

6. What did she long to do when she was in the tree?

   _____

7. Who is Luna? _____

8. What supplies did Julia need? _____

9. How did she get her supplies? _____

10. What did Julia write? _____

11. Why did Julia come down from the tree on December 18, 1999?

    _____

12. What was difficult for her to do when she touched the earth with

    her feet? _____

13. What is the name of the ocean Julia could see?

    _____

14. What town could she see from the tree? _____

15. What disaster could she see from high in the tree?

    _____

 Give Your Opinion

Read these questions. Tell your classmates what you think.

1. Do you think Julia is an eco-terrorist?
2. Would you spend two years of your life in a tree? Why or why not?
3. Do you think Julia did something good?

 Find the Main Ideas

Circle the best answer.

1. Which sentence is the main idea about Julia's home for two years?
   a. Julia lived for two years in comfort in a tree house.
   b. Julia's home was made of redwood.
   c. Julia's home was just a flat piece of wood high in a tree.
   d. Julia built a warm place to live in a redwood tree.

2. What was Julia's reason for spending two years in a tree?
   a. She wanted to stop plans to cut down a forest of old trees.
   b. She liked the thought of living simply.
   c. She wanted to watch the water of the Pacific and the mists.
   d. She wanted to show everyone that it was possible to do it.

3. What is the main idea of Julia's decision to climb the tree?

   a. She wanted to stop the destruction of the trees.

   b. She wanted to show that she could do it.

   c. She wanted to be famous.

   d. She wanted to interview famous people about environmental problems.

 Make Some Inferences

Circle the best answer.

1. Why did Julia have trouble walking?

   a. Her arms were very strong.

   b. She hadn't walked in two years.

   c. She was tired of climbing.

   d. She hadn't eaten good food for a long time.

2. Why did Julia have to climb up 55 meters to put her house into the tree?

   a. That's where her friends were.

   b. She was afraid to be close to the ground.

   c. There were branches there to hold the pieces of wood.

   d. She wanted to see the Pacific from her house.

3. What do environmentalists believe causes mudslides?

   a. the ocean and the fog

   b. only rain and mud on the hills

   c. wet earth and cutting down trees

   d. lumber companies on the land

4. Push-ups and sit-ups are good exercise, but they…

   a. do not help a person stay fit.

   b. are for the legs only.

   c. are not possible to do in a tree.

   d. do not exercise the legs.

5. In the winters, Julia always felt cold because of…
   a. cold temperatures.   c. the snow.
   b. the fog and mist.   d. the branches on the trees.

6. Why is there a lot of fog on the coast of California?
   a. because of the wind and the water of the ocean
   b. because the land is very high and the fog is like clouds
   c. because the climate is hot
   d. because of the magnificent redwood trees

Write Your Thoughts

1. Write a letter to Julia about her reasons for staying in the big redwood tree.
2. Answer the letter you wrote, as if you are Julia.
3. Write a newspaper article for December 11, 1997, about Julia's decision.
4. Write a newspaper story for December 19, 1999.

Let the Boys Sing!

The Boys Choir of Harlem is an expensive program. At a press conference, Dr. Walter Turnbull, director and founder of the choir, and Horace Turnbull, vice president of the choir (on the left), asked for public support of their successful program of working with boys through music.

Prepare to Read

- What is special about boys' singing voices?
- What lessons does a person learn by working with a group?
- How are these lessons important for learning life skills?
- Look at the picture on the first page of this unit. What will you learn about?
- Make a list of your own new words, and try to understand the main ideas.
- Do you get any ideas from the title?

Answer These Questions

First read the story, and then try to answer these questions.

1. Who are the students at the Choir Academy of Harlem?
2. Why did Walter Turnbull give up a career as an opera singer?
3. What does Turnbull teach besides singing?
4. What are the most important lessons at the Choir Academy?

Read the Story

Let the Boys Sing!

1   "A choir is a good starting point for building character,"
says Walter Turnbull. "Since the 14th century, choirs have
been used to educate boys." Turnbull is using the same
method, but with some changes. His boys are inner-city
5   boys. They are also very modern kids. They come from poor
families. Like the other young people around them, they
have to deal with fighting and drugs. Many of them have no
fathers. The brothers and fathers of many others are in
prison. However, if they are students at the Choir Academy
10   of Harlem, they have a special opportunity. Their chances
are better than average.

Walter Turnbull himself came from a fatherless family. He understands from his own experience. His family was very poor, but he managed to get to college. He finished
15 Tougaloo College in Mississippi. Then he went to New York. He earned a master's degree in music from the Manhattan School of Music. He tried to make a career as an opera singer. However, it was hard for a black man. There were very few parts for a black singer. He had no choice but to
20 look for another career. He turned to another love, teaching.

Turnbull had started his first boys' choir at a Harlem church. The people loved the sound of the boys' voices. Turnbull was a very good teacher for the young people. He worked with the children and understood their problems.
25 These children needed help, and he was there to help them. They trusted him too. Turnbull got them help with their lessons. Then he got a counselor for help with their problems. By 1974, there was enough interest to make the boys' choir into a non-profit business. By 1987, it was clear that the
30 choir needed a school. Turnbull started the Choir Academy. Now it is part of the New York Public School System.

Discipline is the center of the academy. Hard work and responsibility are part of the method. Challenges complete the program. Turnbull calls the method of teaching "a classical
35 education." Strong values are part of the curriculum. The boys study German to sing German songs. They study Dutch to sing Dutch songs. They all learn keyboarding, like playing a piano. They have math, science, history, English, and computer classes. The choir practices daily too. They sing from 2:30 to
40 6:30 every day.

"At the choir, we don't tolerate fighting." Turnbull is trying to substitute music for the community in the streets. He believes that music lifts the heart and soul of a person. The boys' lives outside of school can change because of music.

45   Turnbull and Frank Jones, the head of the counseling department, believe that they can help the boys change their lives.

The method that they use starts with finding the right students. Turnbull and Jones try to check every third-grade 50 child in the school district. That's about 3,000 children. At a school, they gather all the third-graders into a room and explain about the choir. Then they spend two minutes with each child. They look for ability, for promise, not skill. They will teach the skill. They also look for children with fire and 55 energy in them. Often these students are troublemakers, but they need energy to succeed at the academy. The program is not an easy one.

From among all the third-grade children, Turnbull and Jones choose 150 children. They invite the parents to a 60 meeting the next week. They expect about one-third of the parents to come. The boys' choir members have to have family support. That support does not mean money. It means belief in the program.

The school year begins in the summer with a three-week 65 camp. They take the boys to a college campus far from the city. Their day starts with exercise at 8:30. Then they begin to sing. The purpose seems to be to learn music, but it is more than that. The lessons that they learn are life lessons. After lunch and swimming, they practice dancing. It helps 70 them develop another part of their music skill.

The discipline is hard, and some boys don't succeed. The rewards are great for those who do. Turnbull's graduates become doctors, teachers, and lawyers. Very few become musicians. The education in a choir isn't only about music.

 **Now go back to *Answer These Questions*.**

Can you answer the questions? If not, then read the story again and continue the lesson. Go back to the questions at the end of the unit. Perhaps you will have answers then.

Learn the New Words

Here are some of the new words and meanings in this reading.

1. an **academy** (noun): a special kind of school
2. **better than average** (idiom): extraordinary
3. to **build character** (idiom): to make better and stronger personality characteristics
4. a **choir** (noun): a group of people who sing together
5. a **classical education** (idiom): the learning in school that follows traditions
6. a **counselor** (noun): a person who gives advice and helps people work out their problems
7. **daily** (adverb): every day
8. **discipline** (non-count noun): the following of strict rules
9. **drugs** (noun plural): chemical substances that change the way a person feels (here, illegal medicines)
10. **fire and energy** (idiom): enthusiasm
11. a **graduate** (noun): a person who has completed the program at a school
12. **inner-city** (adjective): from the center of a city (here, from poor neighborhoods)
13. **keyboarding** (noun): act of using a keyboard such as a computer keyboard or a musical keyboard
14. a **method** (noun): a way to reach a goal
15. a **non-profit business** (idiom): a business with a purpose other than making money
16. a **prison** (noun): a locked place for people who have broken the law
17. a **reward** (noun): a gift that a person earns by doing a good job

18. to **tolerate** (verb): to allow; to accept; to permit

19. a **troublemaker** (noun): a person who causes problems

Practice the New Words

A. Look at the list of new words. Which new words answer these questions?

1. Which three of the new words mean "a person with special characteristics"? _____ _____

   _____

2. Which two new words are words for places?

   _____ _____

3. Which word means "a group of people"? _____

B. Look at the list of new words again. Then read these sentences. Use the correct form of a word from the list to fill in each blank. Words in *italics* are clues to help you. There may be some words that you will use more than once and some that you will not use at all.

1. To use a computer, a person needs some _____ skills.

2. Young people need to work hard, the school director believes, to learn how to follow *directions*. Without _____ that comes from *following rules*, they will not succeed.

3. They practice their music *every day*. They get better because they practice _____ .

4. Students who work hard get the _____ of good grades in school.

5. You might not like other people's ideas, but you must *accept* them. It is important to _____ others' ideas and opinions.

6. Some children seem to *cause problems* in a school. They are the _____ , but they are usually also very intelligent people. They also have a lot of *enthusiasm*, or _____ , which is necessary for success.

7. Most people who break the laws go to _____ .

8. Walter Turnbull turned the boys' choir into a _____ so that he could collect enough money to keep it going.

9. The *school* for the boys' choir is an _____ . The students are young people from _____ New York. New students at the school are _____ in intelligence, but they don't have much discipline.

10. Two men, the school director and the _____ , work with the boys to _____ . Their *way* is a good _____ : they use music to teach discipline.

Find the Details

Skim and scan to find the answers to these questions.

1. How old is the choir method of teaching boys discipline?

   _____

2. Where did Walter Turnbull go to college? _____

3. Where was Turnbull's first boys' choir? _____

4. Who pays for the Choir Academy now? _____

5. What do the boys study at the academy? _____

6. Where do the new students for the academy come from?

   _____

7. How many children are there in the academy school district?

   _____

8. How old are the children who come into the academy? What grade are they in? _____

9. How many new students are asked to come to the Choir Academy every year? _____

10. Who is Frank Jones? _____

11. Why is Frank Jones' job important to the school?

    _____

12. What kind of support do Turnbull and Jones expect from parents?

    _____

Give Your Opinion

Read these questions. Tell your classmates what you think.

1. Do you think that music is a good way to teach discipline?

2. What is difficult about growing up with only one parent at home?

3. Why do you think the school year at the Choir Academy begins with a three-week camp? Do you think it is a good idea? What happens with a group of young people who are together for three weeks?

4. Why do you think troublemakers are good students for the Choir Academy?

Make Some Inferences

Answer these questions.

1. Where is the Choir Academy (which city)? Where is Harlem?

   _____

2. Very few of the boys choose music as a career when they graduate. What are their reasons? Is the music program at the Choir Academy really a waste of time for those boys? _____

3. Why do the boys at Choir Academy have to study languages?

   _____

4. How much singing do the boys do every week?

   _____

5. The community or the "streets" of an inner-city neighborhood are different from other places. Why and how are they different? What are the personal values of many inner-city young people?

   _____

6. What probably happens to a student at the Choir Academy who fights with other students? _____

7. Why do the students learn how to dance? _____

8. How is it possible for inner-city boys to become doctors and lawyers? _____

 Find the Main Ideas

Select the best answer.

1. What is the main idea of the Choir Academy?
   a. Boys can learn to work together and to have discipline by learning to sing together.
   b. A classical education is necessary for boys from an inner-city neighborhood.

c. Walter Turnbull didn't find it easy to be an opera singer, so he
turned to teaching.

d. Learning languages is a good way for a student to develop
thinking skills.

2. What makes a classical education?

a. learning to sing with a group of other people

b learning to work together

c. learning math, science, history, and English

d. learning how to use a computer

3. Which of these titles would work for this story?

a. An Opera Singer Becomes a Teacher

b. Living in Harlem

c. An Extraordinary Boys' Choir

d. A Better-Than-Average Chance

 Write Your Thoughts

1. What were Walter Turnbull's challenges?

2. How do most young people learn to follow rules? How did you
learn discipline?

3. Explain how a choir is a community.

12 Waystation

Martine Colette is the founder and director of the Wildlife Waystation. Martine has "a way" with animals. She tames even wild wolves, like Arizona and Teneya.

Prepare to Read

- Look at the picture on the first page of this unit. What will you learn about?
- Make a list of your own new words, and try to understand the main ideas.
- Do you get any ideas from the title?

Which of these words and ideas will you probably see in this unit? Circle them.

help	fire	animal	care	sick	actor
ranch	music	doctor	ordinary	wild	dogs

Answer These Questions

First read the story, and then try to answer these questions.

1. Who is Martine Colette?
2. What is her special ability?
3. What work does she do now?
4. How does she feel about animals?

Read the Story

Waystation

1   The Wildlife Waystation is a 160-acre ranch in a canyon outside Los Angeles. There are many animals there, well over 1,000. But Waystation isn't an ordinary place in any sense of the word. What is unusual? To start with, the animals

5   are extraordinary. The owner of the ranch is a rare person. And there is nothing usual about the way the animals get there.

     Waystation is home to all kinds of wild animals. There are lions, tigers, bears, wolves, and alligators. There are all kinds of exotic birds and small animals, too. The orangutan at the

10   ranch (his name is Lowell) is a retired actor. These animals

have one thing in common. They were not wanted. Many of them would have been killed. For one reason or another, each of them was in danger. Some of them were sick when they arrived. They get the care of a doctor if they need it. Some of the animals go back to the wild. Others live their lives in peace at the Waystation.

The reason for the Waystation is Martine Colette. This extraordinary woman has a way with animals. She seems to be able to communicate with them. Other people who work with animals think it is a special gift. One person noted, "There can be 10 people trying to move an animal. Martine will go in and talk to the animal. The animal will respond. Somehow, she communicates with them." In addition, the animals trust her. They seem to know that she cares about them. They know that they are safe with her.

Waystation belongs to Martine. She used to work in the entertainment industry as a costume designer. She was very good at her job, and she earned enough to buy the ranch. However, she always loved animals. She took the pets that other people didn't want. Then Lowell needed a home. Then other animals needed her help. Slowly her designing work became less important than the animals. She gave it up to run the Waystation. Other people could design costumes. But there was only one person with her special gift.

Waystation is a shelter, a refuge, a place of safety. For years Martine Colette paid for everything herself. But the costs were rising fast. For example, one tiger cub eats 10 pounds of meat a day. With so many animals to care for, she needed more money. She opened the doors for tours. Many people came to see her with the animals. She plays with the tigers. The wolves are like puppies with her. It was not easy for people to believe! Next she had some fund-raisers. "I'm not comfortable with fund-raisers," she says. But when she is asking for money for the animals, it's different.

45   Waystation is not-for-profit. There is a paid staff of 22 people. There are 35 volunteers who work there full time as well. Most of the $2 million in the budget comes from donations. People give her money simply because they want to help. Martine spends her time taking care of animals and

50 picking up new ones. Many movie stars help her too. They tell others about Waystation. Now, when there is an unusual animal in danger, someone usually calls her. For example, a young bear at Yellowstone Park was in trouble. The bear liked to play with campers' tents. The bear had not hurt anyone,

55 but park officials were concerned. Someone called Martine Colette. She came with her special van and took the bear away to safety.

    Martine truly loves the animals. She enjoys hiking and often takes along a big cat on a leash. Other hikers aren't so

60 sure that they like to walk around with a lion or tiger. But for Martine, it's easy. She is completely comfortable with wild animals. They seem to become tame around her. She would prefer to deal with 25 lions rather than one upset human being. "Dealing with people is the most stressful thing I do,"

65 she says.

Now go back to *Answer These Questions*.

Can you answer the questions? If not, then read the story again and continue the lesson. Go back to the questions at the end of the unit. Perhaps you will have answers then.

Learn the New Words

Here are some of the new words and meanings in this reading.

1. an **acre** (noun): an area of land (0.4 hectare)
2. an **alligator** (noun): a dangerous water animal that lives in Florida and other warm climates
3. a **budget** (noun): a plan for making and spending money
4. to **communicate** (verb): to exchange ideas with words or in other ways
5. a **costume designer** (noun): a person who creates special clothes for actors, singers, and other performers
6. to **deal with** (idiom): to take care of; to manage
7. a **donation** (noun): a gift, usually a gift of money
8. the **entertainment industry** (idiom): the music and movie business
9. **exotic** (adjective): extraordinary; unusual
10. a **fund-raiser** (noun): an event that is planned to make money for a special purpose
11. to **give up something** (idiom): to stop doing something that one likes to do
12. a **leash** (noun): a rope between an animal and the owner's hand
13. an **orangutan** (noun): a monkey-like animal
14. **paid staff** (non-count noun): a group of workers who receive money for their work
15. a **puppy** (noun): a baby animal, usually a baby dog or wolf
16. **retired** (adjective): old enough to stop working and receive money or care
17. a **refuge** (noun): a safe place
18. a **shelter** (noun): a safe place
19. **stressful** (adjective): causing worry; difficult to do
20. a **tour** (noun): an opportunity to walk throughout a place and see it
21. **upset** (adjective): angry; worried; unhappy; not feeling normal

22. a **van** (noun): a large vehicle, bigger than a car and smaller than a truck, with a closed body

23. a **waystation** (noun): a stopping place along a road; a safe resting place

24. a **wolf** (noun): a kind of wild dog-like animal

Practice the New Words

A. Look at the list of new words. Which new words answer these questions?

1. Which three words are animal names? _____

   _____ _____

2. Three of the words mean "a safe place to rest." Which are

   they? _____ _____

   _____

3. One word means "a group of people." Which word is it?

   _____

B. Look at the list of new words again. Then read these sentences. Use the correct form of a word from the list to fill in each blank. Words in *italics* are clues to help you. There may be some words that you will use more than once and some that you will not use at all.

1. A person should try to find a job that is pleasant. A job without

   worries and concerns is always easier than a _____ job.

2. Our dog sees his _____ and knows it is time for a walk.

3. Some birds are *extraordinary* because of their colorful feathers.

   They are _____ birds.

4. A *person who makes the beautiful clothes* for singers is a

   _____ .

5. A famous singer probably needs to have a _____
   for costumes because they cost a lot of *money*.

6. Counselors must know *how to talk with other people* about
   difficult things. They learn to _____ well as
   part of their education.

7. How large is this ranch? Is it more than a 100

   _____ ?

8. The teacher worked in the schools for forty years, but he
   stopped teaching last year. Now he is _____ .

9. Everyone likes to watch a _____ . All babies
   are fun, but *little dogs* make people laugh.

10. She looks *unhappy and angry*. Why is she _____ ?

11. You can carry four or five people in a car and a larger number
    of people in a _____ .

12. The family planned a *trip* around Kenya. They wanted *to see*
    wild animals on their _____ .

13. There are medicines now to help people who want *to stop*
    smoking cigarettes. It's not easy to _____
    smoking.

14. The not-for-profit business asked people for *gifts of money* at
    a *special party*. The party was a _____ , and
    the gifts of money were _____ .

15. Sometimes people don't want to _____ their
   problems. They want to forget them instead.

C. Draw a line between the two words or phrases with similar
   meanings.

1. leash		a. baby
2. shelter		b. gift
3. wolf		c. extraordinary
4. farm		d. monkey
5. tour		e. vehicle
6. orangutan		f. refuge
7. puppy		g. wild dog
8. donation		h. rope
9. van		i. ranch
10. exotic		j. trip

Find the Details

Skim and scan the reading to find the answers to these questions.

1. How large is Martine Colette's ranch? _____

2. Where is her ranch? _____

3. How many people work at the Waystation? _____

4. In what ways does Martine Colette save animals' lives?

   _____

5. Martine Colette had a successful career. What did she do?

   _____

6. Why did she give up her career? _____

7. Who is Lowell? _____

8. How much meat does a tiger cub eat in one day?

   _____

9. What businesses are parts of the entertainment industry?

   _____

10. Why did Martine have to have fund-raisers? How does she feel
    about fund-raisers? _____

11. How large is her budget now? _____

12. How can she take a lion for a walk? How do her neighbors feel
    about a lion on a leash? _____

 ## Give Your Opinion

Read these questions. Tell your classmates what you think.

1. Should Martine Colette take either a lion or a tiger for a walk on
   a leash?
2. Who do you think should take care of animals like those on
   Martine Colette's ranch?
3. Why do you think she can get donations when there are so many
   people who need help and do not get it?
4. Do you believe that Martine Colette can communicate with
   animals? Why or why not? Do you know other people who
   "have a special way with" animals?

 ## Make Some Inferences

Circle all the right answers.

1. Martine Colette's ranch is in a good place because...
   a. it is in a warm climate.
   b. it is near the center of the entertainment industry.
   c. it is near Los Angeles.
   d. it is far from other people and cities.
   e. it is in a canyon.

2. Martine Colette needs a special van because…

    a. she goes to get animals that are in trouble.

    b. she has a lot of paid staff and volunteers.

    c. she needs to pick up animals that are in trouble.

    d. every person needs a vehicle.

3. We know that Martine has a special gift because…

    a. she makes a lot of money.

    b. wild animals trust her.

    c. she seems to be able to communicate with wild animals.

    d. movie stars like her.

    e. people give her money for animals in danger.

    f. she is comfortable with exotic creatures.

 Find the Main Ideas

Select the best answer.

1. The main idea of the Waystation is that…

    a. animals need a safe place to get well or to retire.

    b. animals should be killed when they are not wanted.

    c. everyone needs a pet.

    d. Martine Colette is an extraordinary person.

2. The main idea of a fund-raiser is to…

    a. show people the Waystation.

    b. get gifts of money from interested people.

    c. take people on tours around the ranch.

    d. make up a new budget.

3. A good title for this reading is…

    a. Lions and Tigers

    b. A Bear from Yellowstone

    c. An Interesting Ranch

    d. A Safe Place for Animals

Write Your Thoughts

1. Would you enjoy Martine Colette's kind of life? Why or why not?
2. What special gifts or talents do you have? How do they make you an extraordinary person?

13 Water Logs

Scott Michen rescues logs from the water. The great logs dry slowly in his Wisconsin warehouse.

Prepare to Read

- Where do logs usually come from? Do they usually come from the water?
- Do you know of a great forest?
- Why is forest land valuable?
- Look at the picture on the first page of this unit. What will you learn about?
- Make a list of your own new words, and try to understand the main ideas.
- Do you get any ideas from the title?

Answer These Questions

First read the story, and then try to answer these questions.

1. What is unusual about the logs in this reading?
2. Why are old-growth forests rare now?
3. What is special about the wood in a Stradivarius violin?
4. How has the operation of Superior Water-Logged changed?
5. How is technology making the job of raising the wood easier?

Read the Story

Water Logs

1   Between 1870 and 1910, loggers cut down thousands of trees in the forests of Wisconsin. They piled the logs on huge rafts. Then they sent them down the rivers to the Great Lakes. Two of these lakes border Wisconsin: Lake Michigan

5   and Lake Superior. The logs went to lumber mills (or saw mills) most of the time. However, some rafts of logs became waterlogged (heavy with water) and sank. There were plenty of trees, so no one bothered about the logs on the bottom of the lake. The loggers simply cut more. The forests were great.

10 The trees were many. There was a huge supply.

The Great Lakes, especially Lake Superior, are very cold. The water is also fresh. That is, it contains no salt. Those logs just lie on the bottom of the lake. Some of them were there for 100 years. There is little oxygen down there, so the logs did not rot.

Scott Mitchen was swimming in the lake one day in 1989. He enjoyed diving. He had an oxygen tank on his back, and he was just looking around. He was looking for boats that had sunk. He was about 30 feet from the surface when he saw some logs on the bottom of the bay. They looked interesting to him. He brought the inner tube from a truck tire and filled it with air. He used it to raise his first log. When he cut the log open, he was surprised. The wood was beautiful. It looked like the wood of an antique. This log was, he thought, obviously special wood. And he was right. It is special. It is old-growth wood. It is the result of slow growing. When the forests were natural and thick, all the trees grew slowly. As a result, the wood is very dense. The trees themselves were hundreds of years old.

Mitchen saw an opportunity. He soon went to work on his project. His new hometown needed jobs for its people. So the water-logging business got started. He calls his company Superior Water-Logged. He gets wood from the water of the lakes.

Mitchen talks about working underwater. He says everything down there is gray. The divers move a log, and the mud makes it impossible to see. There is some danger, therefore, from the moving logs and limited visibility. One diver can move a huge log. But sometimes a diver tries to do too much, and he might run out of air. Men who are working underwater don't understand that they might be working too hard.

Mitchen has raised more than 5,000 logs himself. These logs go from the water into an old warehouse. There they sit
45   and dry. Mitchen now has a special oven, a kiln, to dry wood slowly. A log from a lake bottom might be an oak, a maple, or a pine. The hardwoods (like oak and maple) are especially valuable. They are high-quality wood for fine furniture. Mitchen's goal is to find wood good enough to make a fine
50   violin, like the famous violins of Stradivarius. Wood of that quality is very rare. It is more likely to come from water-logged trees than anywhere else. There are not many old-growth forests left on Earth.

The logs themselves have stories to tell. An expert can
55   tell how old a log is by looking at the ends. Axes were used before 1870. It's easy to tell if a log was cut with an ax. After 1870, two-person saws become common. Besides that, many of the logs have stamps on their ends. Like a cattle brand, each stamp gives a lot of information. There were about
60   2,600 different stamps in Wisconsin. A stamp tells who cut the tree. It also tells when the tree was cut.

The water-logging operation has changed considerably. Technology is now important in finding the logs. A computer screen and a sonar machine look for sunken logs. A Global
65   Positioning System can locate a log's position, within a foot or two. Divers go down after the wood. They hammer an eyebolt (a nail with a circle in the head) into a log. They connect it to a cable from the barge on the surface. At a signal, the log is pulled up.

70   Taking logs from the water is becoming big business. Trucks bring in logs from lakes in Canada and states as distant as Georgia and Idaho. Superior Water-Logged has experts for handling this special wood. The company also has many more customers than it can supply.

Now go back to *Answer These Questions*.

Can you answer the questions? If not, then read the story again and continue the lesson. Go back to the questions at the end of the unit. Perhaps you will have answers then.

Learn the New Words

Here are some of the new words and meanings in this reading.

1. an **antique** (noun): an old piece of furniture
2. a **barge** (noun): a boat for carrying a large load
3. to **border** (verb): to be on the edge of; to define the limit of
4. to **bother** (verb): to worry (about or with something)
5. to **contain** (verb): to hold
6. **dense** (adjective): heavy; thick
7. **diving** (noun): swimming deep down into water
8. an **eyebolt** (noun): a nail with a circle in the head
9. a **kiln** (noun): a special kind of oven for slowly heating something wet to dry it out and make it stronger
10. to **lie** (verb): to be located; to rest (past tense = *lie*; past participle = *lain*)
11. **limited** (adjective): having a definite number, few
12. a **logger** (noun): a person who cuts logs as a job
13. **hardwood** (non-count noun and adjective): wood from trees that lose their leaves in the winter (noun), or made from such a tree (adjective)
14. an **inner tube** (noun): the black rubber inside of a car or truck tire

15. (a) **maple** (noun and adjective): a kind of hardwood tree, or made of wood from such a tree

16. a **mill** (noun): a place where wood is cut into lumber

17. (an) **oak** (noun and adjective): type of very hard and heavy tree (noun), or made of wood from such a tree (adjective)

18. **obviously** (adverb): certainly; easily seen

19. an **oven** (noun): an enclosed place for baking; a kiln

20. **oxygen** (non-count noun): the part of air that is necessary for breathing, burning, and rotting

21. **plenty** (non-count noun): lots; more than enough

22. a **raft** (noun): a flat floating craft like a barge that can carry a pile of logs

23. **sonar** (non-count noun) a piece of equipment that uses sound waves to locate things underwater

24. the **surface** (noun): the uppermost layer

25. **visibility** (non-count noun): ability to see

26. a **warehouse** (noun): storage place

27. **water-logged** (adjective): filled with water so that it sinks

Practice the New Words

Look at the list of new words. Then read these sentences. Use the correct form of a word from the list to fill in each blank. Words in *italics* are clues to help you. There may be some words that you will use more than once and some that you will not use at all.

1. A _____ is like an _____ for *baking*
   The difference is that it *heats* the wood slowly and dries it out.

2. Two *kinds of hardwood* are _____ and

   _____ . These trees have very *heavy*,

   _____ wood.

3. Both a _____ and a _____ can *carry*
   logs down a river to a saw _____ to be *cut into*
   lumber.

4. *Inside* a truck *tire* there is an _____ .

5. A person who *cuts down trees* is a _____ .

6. There is not much good heavy wood left in forests, so

   _____ furniture becomes more valuable every day.
   The wood in those *old* pieces is better than most wood that is
   available today.

7. Minnesota, North Dakota, Montana, Idaho, and Washington

   _____ Canada.

8. A log will *float* on the _____ of the water until it

   becomes _____ . Then it *sinks* to the bottom.

9. In the *fog*, it is not easy to see. _____ decreases.

10. The company has a lot of *supplies* in a large _____ .

11. Loggers didn't *worry* about logs that sank. Why _____

    with those logs when there were _____ of trees to
    cut down? There were so *many* trees!

12. An _____ is *similar to a nail, but it has a circle*
    for a rope or strong cable to go through it.

13. People need _____ in air to *breathe.*

14. There are many trees, but you can *count* them. The number of

    trees is _____ .

15. Getting logs out of the water means *swimming* and

    _____ *deep* into the lake.

16. Thousands of logs _____ *on the bottom* of the
    Great Lakes, waiting to be pulled to the surface.

Find the Details

Skim and scan to find the answers to these questions.

1. Who is Scott Mitchen?   _____

2. When in history were the forests of Wisconsin cut down?

   _____

3. What is a lumber mill?   _____

4. Why was Scott Mitchen diving in the cold waters of Lake

   Superior?   _____

5. What did he use to raise the first log?   _____

6. Why didn't the old logs rot in Lake Superior?   _____

7. When is there limited visibility at the bottom of the lake?

   _____

8. How many logs has Mitchen raised himself?   _____

9. What is a Stradivarius? Why is a Stradivarius so valuable?

   _____ _____

10. What information is on a log stamp?   _____

11. How many different log stamps were there in Wisconsin alone?

    _____

12. How does a Global Positioning System help Superior Water-Logged?

    _____

Figure Out the Sequence

What happens first? In the blank in front of each sentence, write a number between 1 and 12 to show what happens next.

a. _____ This log and a lot of other logs go down a river to a lumber mill on Lake Superior.

b. _____ The log is pulled to the surface.

c. _____ A logger cuts down a tree.

d. _____ Superior Water-Logged sends a diver into the water.

e. _____ Sonar or a GPS finds a pile of logs in the water.

f. _____ A stamp is put on the end of the log.

g. _____ A cable is connected to the log on the bottom of the lake.

h. _____ The logs float in the water for a long time, become water-logged, and sink.

i. _____ The diver hammers an eyebolt into the end of the log.

j. _____ About 100 years after the logger cut down the tree, the wood becomes lumber.

k. _____ The hardwood becomes a piece of fine furniture.

l. _____ The log goes to a warehouse and a kiln to dry.

 Give Your Opinion

Read these questions. Tell your classmates what you think.

1. Good business is understanding an opportunity and a need. What do you think of Scott Mitchen's idea? Was it a good business idea? Why or why not?

2. The loggers in Wisconsin between 1870 and 1910 thought the forests were not limited. What do loggers of today think about trees and forest land?

3. Superior Water-Logged is not taking pine trees from the water. Do you think the company will do it in the future? Why or why not?

Make Some Inferences

Read and think about these questions. Then try to answer them.

1. Why are some logs left on the bottom of the lake?

   _____

2. Why does everything become gray in the water when divers are

   working?   _____

3. Why is old-growth wood better than new-growth wood?

   _____

4. What is necessary for wood to rot?   _____

5. Why do divers need oxygen tanks?   _____

6. The wood that comes from the lake bottom is very expensive. It
   costs more than new lumber. Why do customers want it anyway?

   _____

7. Why do water logs come to the Superior Water-Logged warehouses

   from many places other than Lake Superior?   _____

8. What are the two meanings of *water-logged* in this unit?

   _____

 Find the Main Ideas

Select the best answer.

1. What is the main idea behind water-logging?
   a. The bottom of the lake has too many logs on it. It's not good
      for swimming.
   b. Divers need jobs. Therefore, they should bring up the logs.
   c. Valuable trees lie at the bottom of the lake, ready to be used.
   d. A person can look in the water for useful things.

2. What is the main idea about the change in the water-logging operation?

    a. Computers and sonar can help to find valuable logs.

    b. A diver needs to have oxygen in a tank to swim down to the logs on the bottom of the lake.

    c. The loggers of 100 years ago did not have modern technology.

    d. Water-logging is faster and safer with the use of modern equipment.

3. Which title is best for this reading?

    a. A New Business for Scott

    b. Lumber from the Water

    c. Old Logs and New Uses

    d. Technology in Lake Superior

Write Your Thoughts

1. What do you think of a person who takes wood from a lake without asking anyone about it?

2. What does a person need in order to see opportunity in an ordinary thing?

3. What is out of the ordinary about Superior Water-Logged?

14 Whopper

Ken Sullivan started the Liars' Contest because he loves a good story, and he can tell a whopper.

Mike Lantz won the 2001 Liars' Contest with a great story!

Prepare to Read

This unit is about storytellers. Which of these ideas will you probably see in this unit? Write a check (✓) in the blank next to each one

_____ people who tell stories

_____ ideas for new movies

_____ the kinds of stories that people enjoy most

_____ interesting facts about television

_____ stories about people who tell stories

- As you read, make a list of your own new words, and try to understand the main ideas.
- Do you get any ideas from the title? What is a "whopper," anyway?

Answer These Questions

First read the story, and then try to answer these questions.

1. What are the first five paragraphs?
2. What are the reasons for telling stories?
3. Where is Appalachia?
4. a. What is a tale?
   b. What is a joke?
   c. What is a whopper?
   d. What is a lie?
   e. What are the differences among these kinds of stories?

Read the Story

Whopper

1   One day a newspaper reporter was visiting a home for disabled soldiers. He was writing a story about the home and the people who lived there. The director invited him to stay

for dinner. During the dinner, one old soldier got up and
5   shouted out, "Number 55!" The rest of the residents burst
out laughing. A minute or two later, another of the men who
lived there stood up. He had a twinkle in his eye when he said,
in a soft voice, "Number 13!" Again, everyone laughed out
loud. A couple of minutes later, an old soldier in a wheelchair
10   waved his hand. Everyone got quiet. He hollered out,
"Number 200!" Again, the old soldiers laughed and laughed.

     The reporter didn't understand. He turned to the director.
"What are they doing?" he asked.

     "Well," the director answered, "they all know the same
15   funny stories. They decided to number them to save time. So
they use just the number of the joke."

     "Oh," said the reporter. He thought a moment, and then
he stood up. "Number 92!" he shouted. The residents looked
at him. No one laughed. He sat down, red-faced.

20   The director looked at him with sad eyes. "Some people
just can't tell a story," he said.

     The tradition of storytelling is as old as people. Before
television and radio, before books and electric light, there
were storytellers. Parents and grandparents have always told
25   stories to their children. Stories can teach lessons, and they
entertain. Stories keep alive some of the great events in
history. They help families understand who they are too. In
some places, not much storytelling goes on anymore, but it
is not so everywhere. The tradition of stories is alive and well
30   in the mountains of West Virginia. In the Appalachian area,
stories have always been a lively part of community life. In
the evenings, in homes, at a church hall, or at the general
store, men, women, and children would gather around a
storyteller, and they would listen to tales. Many of the stories
35   of Appalachia are about an average person. This ordinary

person (the hero of the story) outwits a person of greater strength. There are stories about fishing and stories about visitors from other worlds. The stories aren't true, of course. They are very, very funny lies! Some of these stories are truly

40   whoppers!

Ken Sullivan has always loved a good story. He loves to tell stories and to listen to them. "One of the deepest human needs is the need for a story," Sullivan says. A story can be funny or scary. It can be inspiring, like stories about courage

45   or loyalty. A good story helps people make sense out of the world. Sullivan worried that television was taking over for storytelling, so he did something about it. He started West Virginia's annual Liars Contest. Every year since 1983, at the end of May, there has been a storytelling contest in Charleston.

50   A standing-room-only crowd gathers at the Cultural Center to hear the best stories of the year.

Each contestant has about five minutes to tell his or her story. Most stories have a little bit of truth to them. In fact, a good story always starts out with human experience. A good

55   story starts with something familiar. Then the storyteller figures out what's funny about it. A funny idea is not enough. There is skill is being a good storyteller.

According to Tom Drummond, who has won many Liars Contests, "A good tale is like a song. If you don't sing it right,

60   it doesn't work." Bill Lepp has won too. All his stories are about his dog Buck. Buck is a hunting dog, a good dog. But Buck has one problem. He's afraid of guns. You can imagine why Buck stories are whoppers.

Bonnie Collins is a judge for the Liars Contest. "When I
65   was a child, stories were our fun. Maybe you already knew
a story, but it got better and better every time." The 85-year-
old loves a good story. "You have to have a knack for telling
a story," she says. "Some people can tell a story, and some
people can't."

Now go back to *Answer These Questions.*

Can you answer the questions? If not, then read the story again and
continue the lesson. Go back to the questions at the end of the unit.
Perhaps you will have answers then.

Learn the New Words

Here are some of the new words and meanings in this reading.

1. **Appalachia** (proper noun): the mountain region in West Virginia
2. to **be alive and well** (idiom): to continue to live; to thrive
3. a **contest** (noun): a competition in which people try to win a prize
4. a **contestant** (noun): a person who participates in a contest
5. **disabled** (adjective): handicapped; not fully capable
6. to **entertain** (verb): to make people laugh and enjoy themselves
7. an **event** (noun): a happening
8. to **have a knack** (idiom): to have a special talent or ability
9. to **have a twinkle in one's eye** (idiom): an expression on one's face that lets people know that one is telling a funny lie or a joke
10. a **hero** (noun): the main character in a story
11. to **holler** (verb): to call in a loud voice
12. **inspiring** (adjective): said of an idea that makes people feel good about themselves
13. a **joke** (noun): a short funny story
14. to **keep alive** (idiom): to help continue
15. a **liar** (noun): a person who tells a story that is not true

16. to **lie** (verb): to tell something that is not true

17. **lively** (adjective): entertaining; full of energy; fast-moving; active

18. to **make sense out of** (idiom): to understand

19. to **outwit** (verb): to trick; to be smarter than

20. **red-faced** (adjective): embarrassed

21. a **resident** (noun): a person who lives at a place

22. **scary** (adjective): frightening

23. a **soldier** (noun): a person who fights for his or her country

24. **standing-room-only crowd** (idiom): the audience of a theater performance to which all tickets are sold

25. a **tale** (noun): a story

26. a **wheelchair** (noun): a movable chair for a person who cannot walk easily

27. a **whopper** (noun): a story that is very funny and obviously not true

Practice the New Words

A. Look at the list of new words. Which new words answer these questions?

1. Which five words are words for people? _____

_____ _____ _____

_____

2. Which three words are stories? _____

_____ _____

3. Which word is a place named after some mountains?

_____

B. Look at the list of new words again. Then read these sentences. Use the correct form of a word from the list to fill in each blank. Words in *italics* are clues to help you. There may be some words that you will use more than once and some that you will not use at all.

1. You need a loud voice to _____ .

2. People tell funny stories to teach lessons and to _____ other people because everyone enjoys a good laugh.

3. Some people have a special way of telling stories that makes them very funny. They _____ for storytelling.

4. You can always tell when that old man is going to tell a _____ . He gets a _____ in his eye.

5. What kind of story do you like best—an _____ tale about courage, a _____ story that will give you bad dreams, or a _____ that will make you laugh?

6. Who will win the storytelling _____ this year? There are ten people in this year's event, and every one of these _____ has good stories to tell.

7. At the university, there is a special door in every building for students who don't walk and who use _____ .

8. If one person is smarter than another, he or she will _____ the other person.

9. I wanted to learn to speak another language, but at first it wasn't easy for me. After about two weeks, however, I began to understand how the language worked. In other words, I began to _____ it.

10. I wanted to go to the show, but there were no tickets left for seats in the theater. It was a _____ !

11. There are some kinds of dancing that could die out. However, there are clubs that _____ those traditions.

12. The Charleston _____ Contest happens every May. This _____ takes place at the Cultural Center. The stories that win prizes are usually _____ .

13. There are 120 people who live in this dormitory. The _____ are students at the college.

14. People in the army are _____ .

15. The band played a _____ song, so people got up to dance. They enjoyed the quick, fast-moving music.

C. Read this short list of words. Then write the word that goes with each of the numbered items.

> to lie   outwit   disabled   red-faced   contestant

1. a person in a wheelchair   _____

2. a person in a dance contest   _____

3. a liar   _____

4. a person who made a mistake   _____

5. what a smart person can do   _____

Find the Details

Skim and scan to find the answers to these questions.

1. Why do parents tell stories to their children?   _____

2. Where is Appalachia?   _____

3. What buildings were likely to be centers for a community in an Appalachian town?   _____

4. What three purposes are mentioned for the tradition of telling

   stories? _____ _____ _____

5. Where is the Cultural Center? _____

6. How much time does each storyteller have during the contest?

   _____

7. What is the center of every good story? _____

8. What's wrong with Bill Lepp's hunting dog? _____

Give Your Opinion

Read these questions. Tell your classmates what you think.

1. Why do some stories get better with each telling?
2. Why are some people good storytellers and other people don't
   have the knack?
3. How long is a good story in your opinion?
4. What do you think of the name of the contest, the Liars Contest?
5. Is there something extraordinary about a good storyteller? What
   is it?

Make Some Inferences

Circle all the right answers.

1. The hero of most stories is an ordinary person who does
   extraordinary things because...
   a. most listeners are ordinary people.
   b. listeners want the smart one to be outwitted by someone like
      them.
   c. it makes the story better.
   d. people like a story that has some truth to it.
   e. there are no extraordinary people in West Virginia.
   f. that is the tradition of storytelling in Appalachia.

2. Bonnie Collins is probably a good judge for the Liars Contest because...

   a. she has heard many good storytellers tell their stories.

   b. she is quite old.

   c. she is probably a good storyteller herself.

   d. she has a lot of experience with listening to stories.

   e. she remembers a lot of stories from her childhood.

   f. she loves to hear a whopper.

   g. she understands that some people have the knack of storytelling and some do not.

 ## Analyze This Joke

A good joke ends with a *punch line*. Some stories have more than one punch line. What do you think about punch lines in this story?

> Tony and Leo were putting new pieces of wood on the outside of a house. Tony was very strong with a hammer, but he was throwing away a lot of nails. Leo asked, "Hey, Tony. Why are you throwing away all those nails?"
>
> Tony, who wasn't very smart, answered. "The heads of those nails are on the wrong end."
>
> Leo laughed, "Oh, Tony! Didn't you know? Those nails are for the other side of the house."

 ## Find the Main Ideas

Select the best answer.

1. What is the main idea of the joke that begins the reading?

   a. Some people can tell a story well, and other people don't have the knack.

   b. All jokes have numbers.

   c. Most newspaper reporters don't have a clue about what is really funny.

   d. Old soldiers enjoy a good story.

2. What is the main idea of telling a good story?

   a. A good story must be about an average person in an unusual situation.

   b. A good story has to be about extraordinary events.

   c. A good story needs to be told fast.

   d. A story is as good as the storyteller.

3. Which of these titles fits the reading?

   a. Life in Appalachia Today

   b. The Appalachian Tradition of Storytelling

   c. Tom Drummond's Contest

   d. Stories Alive and Well in West Virginia

Write Your Thoughts

1. Think of a joke or a tale and write it. Then read it to your classmates.

2. Analyze a joke. Why is it funny?

3. Analyze an inspiring story. What makes it a good story?

15 Hummers

Hummingbirds are tiny and fast. Their wings don't stop when they pause to eat.

Prepare to Read

This unit is about some very small birds. Which of these ideas will you probably see in this unit? Write a check (✓) in the blank next to each one.

_____ what the birds are called

_____ where the birds sleep

_____ what the birds eat

_____ what they look like

_____ what their scientific name is

_____ why they are interesting

_____ how they are different from other birds

- Make a list of your own new words, and try to understand the main ideas.
- Do you understand the title? Why don't you get any ideas from the title?

Answer These Questions

First read the story, and then try to answer these questions.

1. Where do hummingbirds live?
2. How did they get their name?
3. What do they eat?
4. Where do they go in the winter? Why?
5. What is unusual about hummingbirds?

Read the Story

Hummers

1   "I think time is different for hummingbirds," said Joyce, an enthusiastic birdwatcher. She watched a broadtail as it squealed through the air. The heart of an average hummingbird beats 1,200 times a minute. Its wings hum at 2,280 revolutions

5   a minute. They go so fast that their wings make a squealing sound as they fly. The tiny bird breathes 250 times a minute. Hummingbirds seem to live faster than any other bird.

Hummingbirds are an American species. There are no hummers in other parts of the world. Furthermore, they are 10   good tourists. They visit almost every part of North America over the course of a year. Most hummers spend the winter in Mexico and fly north to Canada and Alaska in the summer months. Hummers eat flower nectar, and they love mountain meadows. The many flowers are hummingbird heaven.

15   Rich in color, from red to purple, hummingbirds interest many. A great deal of information has been learned about them. For example, there are 320 kinds of hummingbirds in North America. The bee hummingbird, from Cuba, is the smallest. It weighs less than a dime. The rufous and the 20   broadtail weigh less than a nickel. People think that they are cute because they are so small. And they are so sweet. After all, they love flowers. They are like tiny fairies, little magical creatures.

However, hummingbird life is not all pleasant. They fight 25   one another for food. A typical male sits and guards its food all day. He doesn't eat until evening, however. If he did, he would not be able to fly fast to chase other hummingbirds from its flowers.

The male will fly after other birds 40 times an hour. In 30   displays of power, a male hummingbird will fly straight up 60 feet. Then he turns and swoops down in a terrifying squeal of wings. The male waits until evening to eat. Then he eats for 20 minutes straight. Its weight increases by a third. And he has what he needs to live through a cold night.

35   Female hummers feed all day. They have to carry the thick nectar back to their babies. At the nest, the babies open

their mouths, and the mother puts its long beak down in. She packs the food into the babies. They gain eight times their weight in two weeks. Life goes fast for hummers.

40   The brain of a hummingbird is the size of a tack head. Yet these tiny brains remember where flowers are, from year to year. People put out hummingbird feeders, filled with sugar water. And the birds come back to look for them, year after year. If the human being doesn't put out the feeder, the

45   birds complain. Their shrill sounds and the chirps remind the human beings of their responsibility to provide food. The birds fly north and south along bird highways. People who live along their route know that they will come. One man near the Mexican border puts up 150 hummingbird feeders

50   every year. He buys as much as 150 pounds of sugar a week. Those birds, he says, are hungry! And about 10,000 a day stop for a snack.

A hummingbird needs from seven to twelve calories a day to survive. A teaspoon of sugar has 15 calories in it. That

55   doesn't seem like much, but just figure it out. An average man weighs about 170 pounds. If a hummingbird weighed that much, it would be eating 170 pounds of meat a day. To get enough food in a day, a hummingbird must find about 1,000 flowers a day. It drinks twice its weight in nectar every day.

60   The hummingbird is truly an unusual bird. Its only goal seems to be survival. And the birds that fly the fastest are the strongest. They are the ones that live for another year.

Now go back to *Answer These Questions.*

Can you answer the questions? If not, then read the story again and continue the lesson. Go back to the questions at the end of the unit. Perhaps you will have answers then.

Learn the New Words

Here are some of the new words and meanings in this reading.

1. a **beak** (noun): a part of a bird that works like mouth and nose

2. a **birdwatcher** (noun): a person who enjoys watching birds as a hobby

3. **cute** (adjective): small and pretty

4. a **dime** (noun): a small silver 10-cent coin in U.S. or Canadian money

5. a **display** (noun): a show; a demonstration

6. **enthusiastic** (adjective): full of energy; enjoying with good will

7. a **feeder** (noun): a piece of equipment for giving food to animals

8. to **gain** (verb): to increase in amount or value

9. a **hummer** (noun): another word for *hummingbird*

10. a **hummingbird** (noun): a kind of small bird that eats flower nectar and makes a humming sound as it flies

11. to **increase** (verb): to become larger or greater in number

12. **nectar** (non-count noun): the sweet juice inside a flower

13. a **nickel** (noun): a 5-cent coin in U.S. or Canadian money, larger and heavier than a dime

14. **power** (non-count noun): strength and ability

15. a **revolution** (noun): one complete circular turn

16. a **route** (noun): a familiar road; a way

17. **shrill** (adjective): said of a high, sharp sound

18. a **snack** (noun): a small meal; something to eat

19. to **squeal** (verb): to make a high, sharp sound

20. **survival** (non-count noun): act of staying alive

21. to **swoop down** (idiom): to fly down from a high point to catch something or chase something

22. a **tack** (noun): a small, nail-like object with a wide head, used to put papers on a bulletin board

23. **terrifying** (adjective): frightening; scary

Practice the New Words

A. Look at the list of new words. Then read these sentences. Use the correct form of a word from the list to fill in each blank. Words in *italics* are clues to help you. There may be some words that you will use more than once and some that you will not use at all.

1. I don't have much *money* with me, just some coins—a

   _____ and a few thin _____ .

2. The car stopped with a _____ of the brakes.

   The _____ *sound* hurt my ears.

3. The teacher needs some _____ to put students'

   pictures on the wall. She is making a _____ of

   art work to show what the students can draw.

4. The airplane was *flying high in the sky*, but then it

   _____ close to the ground to drop water on the

   forest fire.

5. Some people are _____ about all kinds of birds.
   They love to *watch* them and *feed* them. The people are

   _____ , and they put food into _____

   for the birds to eat.

6. The _____ of a hummingbird is long and thin.
   That's why it can reach deep into flowers to *drink* the sweet

   _____ .

7. The *humming sound* of a _____ comes from

   the _____ of its wings as it flies. That sound is

   _____ to other hummingbirds. It *frightens* them

   away.

8. Which is the best road to St. Louis from here? Is it a truck

    _____ ?

9. How does a male _____ show its _____

    _____ ? By some fancy flying! It takes a lot of

    strength to fly that way. The reward for hummingbirds that fly

    fast is _____ .

10. A hummingbird eats enough nectar in twenty minutes to

    _____ its weight by a third. Baby hummingbirds

    _____ eight times their weight in two weeks.

B. Draw a line between the two words or phrases with similar
meanings.

1. hummingbird heaven	a. live
2. fairy	b. gain
3. highway	c. something to eat
4. nectar	d. hummingbird
5. survive	e. coin
6. snack	f. mountain meadows
7. shrill sound	g. route
8. nickel	h. squeal
9. increase	i. sugar water
10. hummer	j. magical creature

Find the Details

Skim and scan to find the answers to these questions.

1. What is the average hummingbird's heartbeat rate (how many
   times per minute)? _____

2. Why do hummingbirds make that squealing sound? How do they
   do it? _____

3. How many times per minute does a hummingbird breathe?

   _____

4. In the reading, find the names of three kinds of hummingbirds.

   _____ _____ _____

5. How many kinds of hummingbirds are there in North America?

   _____

6. When do female and male hummingbirds eat? Why are their eating patterns different? _____

7. What are fairies? Why do hummingbirds make people think of fairies? _____

8. How large is the brain of a hummingbird? _____

9. How fast does a baby hummingbird grow? How much in two weeks? Why? _____

10. How many flowers does a hummingbird stop at each day?

   _____

11. How many calories in food does a hummingbird need each day?

   _____

12. How do male hummingbirds display their power?

   _____

13. Where in the world are there hummingbirds? _____

14. Where is the smallest hummingbird from? _____

Give Your Opinion

Read these questions. Tell your classmates what you think.

1. Do you think hummingbirds are cute and sweet? Why or why not?
2. Do you think time is different for hummingbirds? Why or why not?
3. How would you feel about hummingbirds if they were 100 times as large as they are? Why?

Make Some Inferences

Read and think about these questions. Then try to answer them.

1. Why do hummingbirds like mountain meadows?

   _____

2. Why is the Cuban hummingbird called *the bee hummingbird?*

   _____

3. Why does it seem that time must be different for hummingbirds?

   _____

4. "Hummingbirds are good tourists." What does this statement

   mean?   _____

5. Hummingbirds need their long thin beaks. Why?

   _____

6. How do we know that hummingbirds have good memories?

   _____

7. Why do male hummingbirds guard hummingbird feeders with

   sugar water in them?   _____

8. The seven to twelve calories that a hummingbird needs are equal

   to how many calories for a 170-pound man?   _____

9. How many calories are there in one teaspoon of sugar?

   _____

10. Which hummingbirds survive?   _____

Find the Main Ideas

A. Write a check (✓) in the blank next to each title that will work for this reading.

_____ A Fast Life

_____ Birdwatcher's Heaven

_____ Fast Flyers

_____ Hummingbirds in Heaven

_____ Hummers: A North American Species

_____ Long, Narrow Beaks

_____ Cuban Hummingbirds

_____ Cute Little Fairies

_____ The North American Hummingbird Route

_____ The Flowers of North America

B. Write a check (✓) in the blank next to each sentences from the reading that seems like the main idea.

_____ Hummingbirds are an American species.

_____ However, hummingbird life is not all pleasant.

_____ In displays of power, a male hummingbird will fly straight up 60 feet.

_____ Its only goal seems to be survival.

_____ At the nest, the babies open their mouths, and the mother puts its long beak down in.

_____ The birds fly north and south along bird highways.

Write Your Thoughts

1. What evidence do you see that hummingbirds have good memories? Make a list of the ideas.

2. Life for the male and female hummingbirds follows different patterns. Write a daily schedule for each bird.

3. Why do you think people find hummingbirds so interesting?

4. What are the personal qualities of a birdwatcher? Do you like to watch birds?

5. Some biologists do research on birds. They study hummingbirds, too. What have they learned about these tiny birds? Write a summary of what they have learned. Use the information in this reading for your summary.

16 Where Did Drake Stop?

Drake's boat was a sailing ship like this one.

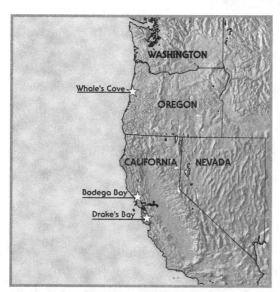

This map of the western coast of the United States shows three possible landing places for Drake's ship, the *Golden Hind*.

Prepare to Read

- Look at the map and the picture on the first page of this unit. What will you learn about?
- What does the map show?
- Make a list of your own new words, and try to understand the main ideas.
- This reading concerns one sea voyage. What do you learn from the map?
- Do you get any ideas from the title?

Answer These Questions

First read the story, and then try to answer these questions.

1. How old is the map?
2. Who was Drake?
3. One group of people loved him, and another group hated him. To one group he was a hero. To the other, he was a pirate. Explain.
4. Why is there so much argument about his trip in modern times?

Read the Story

Where Did Drake Stop?

1   Francis Drake, an Englishman, was the second ship captain to circumnavigate the Earth. That is, he sailed all the way around. (And, unlike Magellan, the first, he lived to tell the tale.) Records of his voyage tell the details of the long trip by

5   sea. Records include details of an American landing. In June of 1579, Drake's tiny ship stopped somewhere on the western coast of North America. That was 16 years before the first British colony on American soil. It was a cold day, but Drake decided to stay for a while. He and his men had just crossed

10   the thousands of miles of Pacific Ocean. It probably felt good

to be on land. And the small *Golden Hind* needed repairs. Drake and his sailors found the climate pleasant. The local people were friendly. The English sailors built a place to stay on land. And they called the land "Nova Albion," or New

15   England. They wrote in the records that they left a brass plate to show that they were there. On the plate are the words *Francis Drake* and *Nova Albion*. This group of Englishmen stayed for more than five weeks. And then they got on the *Golden Hind* again, and they sailed, this time around South

20   America. Eventually they reached home in England.

Francis Drake was a hero in England. Queen Elizabeth I was queen, and she was very happy with Francis Drake. Drake was really a pirate. He stole gold from the Spanish. He was a thief on the seas. But he gave all the gold to his queen.

25   His sailors were told not to talk about the trip. It was to be a secret. He didn't want the Spanish to know about the stop in North America. He didn't want anyone to know about the riches there, either.

According to Drake's ship records, he stopped at about

30   38 degrees latitude. Was that the truth? Or did he write that number to confuse the Spanish? If it was the truth, then Drake probably stopped on the California coast. There is a drawing of Drake's harbor. Unfortunately, it doesn't help much. The picture looks like every bay or cove on the Pacific

35   coast from Mexico to Canada.

People who are interested in history like to study famous people. These history buffs (that's what they are called) write about the food, the clothes, and the trips. They really want to figure out where Drake and his men stopped. That's

40   why so many theories have developed. Everyone agrees that the *Golden Hind* pulled into a harbor on the North American coast. They know that it was June and that the day was cold.

Could it have been Mexico in June? The weather there in June is usually not cold, so Mexico is probably not the place.

45 They agree on that much, but not about much else. Each group of history buffs has its own theory. And they can become very emotional about it.

"It's like an old mystery story or a jigsaw puzzle. And a lot of the pieces are missing," says one Drake detective.

50 Everyone wants to find the metal plate with Drake's name and *Nova Albion* on it. In the 1930s, someone actually found such a brass plate. It was given to a library at the University of California. But 50 years later, some professional scientists tested the plate. They proved that the plate was a fake. The

55 brass was new brass, 20th century metal. In other words, the plate was made in the 20th century. And the arguments about which bay began all over again.

It is interesting that there is so much detective work. History buffs look for signs of a building. They try to figure

60 out how Drake figured out the location. Some people think that the place was Bodega Bay. Others think that it was Whale's Cove in Washington State. Others put the site more to the north, near Vancouver. Those amateur historians have quite a discussion going. They are writing books about their

65 beliefs, and they have Web sites, too. One said that it would be a shame if someone found the real metal plate. Then all the detective work would be over. The fun would be over too.

 Now go back to *Answer These Questions*.

Can you answer the questions? If not, then read the story again and continue the lesson. Go back to the questions at the end of the unit. Perhaps you will have answers then.

Learn the New Words

Here are some of the new words and meanings in this reading.

1. **amateur** (adjective): not professional
2. an **argument** (noun): a war or battle of words
3. to **circumnavigate** (verb): to sail all the way around
4. a **colony** (noun): a group of people who live together far from their homeland
5. to **confuse** (verb): to mix up; to cause to make a mistake
6. a **cove** (noun): a protected inlet or bay
7. a **detective** (noun): a person, usually from a police force, who investigates crimes or looks for evidence
8. **emotional** (adjective): full of feeling; expressing feelings
9. a **fake** (noun): a phony; something not real
10. to **feel good** (verb): to feel healthy; to feel that everything is fair
11. a **history buff** (noun): a person who loves history and is deeply interested in it
12. a **jigsaw puzzle** (noun): a picture on heavy cardboard cut into pieces to be put back together
13. a **landing** (noun): a time of coming onto shore from a boat or ship
14. **latitude** (non-count noun): measurement of how far north or south
15. a **metal plate** (noun): a thin, flat piece of metal on which words can be written
16. a **pirate** (noun): a thief on the sea in a ship who takes from other ships
17. **records** (noun plural): information about times, schedules, places, and so on
18. to **sail** (verb): to travel by ship or boat
19. a **secret** (noun): information that is not to be told to anyone else
20. a **shame** (noun): something people are sorry about
21. **soil** (non-count noun): the ground; the earth; land (not the sea)
22. a **theory** (noun): an idea that is not proven
23. a **voyage** (noun): a trip in a ship on an ocean or on a sea

⊞ Practice the New Words

A. Look at the list of new words. Then read these sentences. Which word from the list fits in each blank? Words in *italics* are clues to help you. There may be some words that you will use more than once and some that you will not use at all.

1. Ferdinand Magellan was a Portuguese sailor. He started *a long trip by ship* for the king of Spain in 1521. This _____ was to start in Spain and end in Spain. His plan was to *go all the way around the world*—to _____ the world. Magellan died before the end of the trip. His ships, however, _____ all the way home to Spain.

2. Children often enjoy *putting together the many parts* of a _____ , especially if the *picture* is pleasing to them.

3. People who *enjoy studying history* are _____ historians. They study *old reports* and ship _____ to learn about events of the past. These _____ don't know exactly what happened, but they can make _____ about how events could have happened. They become history _____ as they *look for evidence* to support their ideas about past events. Evidence makes their _____ stronger.

4. History books state that the first group of people from England came to the North American coast in 1595. They tried to start a _____ on the east coast, but their *little community* was not successful.

5. The Spanish said that Drake was a thief, a _____ . To the English, he was a hero.

6. There are *some genuine* old coins in the collection, but some of the coins are _____ , not real.

7. A _____ is *a natural harbor*. Drake and his men made a _____ on North American _____ in June 1579. The exact place *where they stepped off the boat and onto land* was a _____ . Drake told his men *not to talk about* the trip because he didn't want the Spanish to know about it. The ship records mention 38 degrees _____ .

8. A person usually _____ after a full night of sleep.

9. There are many numbers in this report. So many numbers _____ me. I *don't think the report is easy to understand.*

10. Magellan was a brave man, but he was killed on the voyage. It was a _____ that he didn't get back to Spain.

B. Draw a line between the two words or phrases with similar meanings.

1. thief
2. history buff
3. sail around
4. voyage
5. theory
6. community
7. records
8. cove
9. soil
10. latitude

a. colony
b. north and south
c. reports and schedules
d. possible explanation
e. pirate
f. amateur historian
g. land
h. trip by ship
i. circumnavigate
j. bay

Find the Details

Skim and scan to find the answers to these questions.

1. Who was the first ship captain to sail around the world?

    _____

2. How was Sir Francis Drake more successful than that first one?

    _____

3. What was the name of Drake's ship?   _____

4. According to the records of the voyage, when did Drake's ship land

    on the western coast of North America?   _____

5. According to the voyage records, where did Drake's ship land on

    the western coast of North America? What part of the coast is at

    that point? Why aren't people sure of the landing place?

    _____

6. What happened in 1930 that is important to the story of Drake's

    stop in North America?   _____

7. What was proved to be a fake?   _____

8. Where is Whale's Cove?   _____

9. Why do the Drake detectives, those history buffs, look for signs of

    a building in the many coves of the Pacific?   _____

10. Every history buff hopes to be the person to find the missing

    metal plate, and yet they all hope it will never be found. Why?

    _____

Give Your Opinion

Read these questions. Tell your classmates what you think.

1. What is your opinion of history buffs who get emotional about events of almost 500 years ago?

2. Do you think Sir Francis Drake should be considered a hero? Why or why not?

3. Why did someone put a 20th century brass plate in the ground with Drake's name and *Nova Albion* on it? What do you think of the person who did it?

 Make Some Inferences

Read and think about these questions. Then try to answer them.

1. Queen Elizabeth I made Francis Drake a knight because to her he was a hero. What do you think of Sir Francis Drake? What did the Spanish king think of Francis Drake?

2. In what year did scientists determine that the metal plate was a fake?

3. How did history buffs feel after it became clear that the metal plate was a fake?

4. Why are the weather reports and the date that they landed on the North American shore important to history buffs?

5. History buffs look for evidence of old buildings in many of the bays on the Pacific coast. Why is their job likely to be a difficult one?

 Find the Main Ideas

Select the best answer.

1. The main reason for stopping in North America was that…

    a. the men wanted to rest after crossing the Pacific Ocean.

    b. the local people were very friendly.

    c. the weather was pleasant, and the beach looked nice too.

    d. the ship needed repairs.

2. The main reason Drake was a hero in England is that he...

    a. brought gold to the queen.

    b. named the new lands "Nova Albion."

    c. was a pirate.

    d. was the captain of the *Golden Hind*.

3. The main reason Drake's records might not be the truth is that...

    a. he didn't have a way to measure latitude well.

    b. he might have wanted to confuse the Spanish.

    c. his trip was a secret.

    d. one of the sailors might have made a mistake in the records.

4. Choose the title that gives the main idea for the reading.

    a. A Pirate Captain

    b. Mystery Bay

    c. History Buffs and Sir Francis Drake

    d. At 38 Degrees Latitude

Write Your Thoughts

1. Are you a history buff? If you are, what part of history is most interesting to you? Why?

2. The stories about Sir Francis Drake are "romantic" because he did so many extraordinary things. He stole gold from the Spanish. He sailed around the world. He found gold and took it to England. Write about one of the extraordinary things he did.

3. Write a letter to the person who put a fake metal plate in the ground near a bay in California. What is your opinion of this person? Why do you think the person did it?

Junkyard Engineer

Charlie Britton uses the old to make new instruments.

Charlie's materials must be well organized so that he can find what he needs.

Prepare to Read

- Do you tend to save things, thinking that you might need them?
- What do you all these saved things? Are they really valuable? Or are they junk? When is it junk? And when is it a valuable resource?
- Do the pictures on the first page of this unit give you some ideas about junk? What do you think you will learn about?
- Make a list of your own new words, and try to understand the main ideas.
- Do you get any ideas from the title?

Which of these words and ideas will you probably see in the unit? Circle them.

junk   animals   information about cities   students

libraries   students   ideas about teaching   a laboratory

Make a list of your own ideas here:

_____ _____ _____

_____ _____ _____

Answer These Questions

First read the story, and then try to answer these questions.

1. Who is Charlie Britton?
2. Where does he work?
3. What does he collect? Why?
4. Why does a university need a person like Charlie?
5. What is a prototype?

Read the Story

Junkyard Engineer

1   Charlie Britton collects junk. He looks through all the equipment that anyone at his university wants to throw away. "I'm a junkyard dog, "he admits. "If it's flat or round

and not too full of holes, we'll take it." Britton and his part-time
assistant, Greg Florian, work in a science lab. They work for
any scientist who needs something special. They charge $25
an hour. They add the cost of supplies, if they have to buy
them. Their idea is not to have to buy anything.

People who do research sometimes need some rather
unusual things. One professor needed to measure the blood
pressure of frogs. Charlie and Greg made a miniature blood
pressure cuff. Another research project involved an exercise
bicycle. The researcher wanted to be able to measure oxygen
use. So Charlie and Greg built a special exercise bicycle. It
measures the oxygen of the person who is riding on the
bicycle. The two men are interested in recycling water. So they
have also made a model for treatment of wastewater. Charlie
builds many prototypes, or models. Perhaps a professor wants
to know if an idea will work. He asks Charlie. Charlie goes
through the junk on his storeroom shelves, and like a junkyard
dog, he "sniffs out" whatever is needed. Together, Charlie, his
assistant, and sometimes the professor build a working model
and test it for almost no cost.

Charlie responds to special department requests. The
biology department has several large greenhouses for plant
experiments. However, some researchers wanted to do an
experiment about sunshine needs of different plants. They
needed to control the amount of sunshine. To limit the sunshine
in a campus greenhouse, Charlie and Greg figured out a way to
make a greenhouse shield.

Of course, there are science laboratory companies. They
make all kinds of lab equipment. So some of this kind of
equipment is available from supply houses. However, it can
be very expensive. It can also take a long time for equipment
to be shipped from a supply house. Charlie and Greg believe

in saving money. The university does too. The two men also believe in working fast. They can respond to requests in just a few days. Their lab has a big storehouse. It looks like a jumble of discarded equipment. There are old shelves and
40   bed frames. There are hoses and glass. There are plastic tubes and plastic tubs. There are wires and cables of all kinds. They can find other pieces at local hardware stores.

Britton added up the projects that he has worked on. In nine years, he had completed 950 special projects. He keeps
45   a record of the supply house costs of these projects. He says that they would have cost the scientists $350,000 to buy. And some of the equipment, like the blood pressure cuffs for frogs, is simply not available. The result of the work is that the scientists have more money to spend on their experiments.

50   A physics professor said, "We scientists are independent people. We tend to like to work on our own." Therefore, science researchers might check in a catalog for prices. They might get ideas of how to put together a piece of equipment. They might even draw plans for the needed piece of equipment.
55   The physics professor continued, "First I figure out what I need. Then I take my ideas to Charlie. He makes the experiment possible by making what I need."

Charlie Britton is truly a junkyard engineer. He knows how to put things together. His skill is understanding "flow."
60   That is, he can look at a picture and understand the starting point, the steps, and the result. His challenge is to find a way to make the equipment. He always looks for a way to use the junk in his storeroom to assemble a machine or a gadget that will do the job.

Now go back to *Answer These Questions.*

Can you answer the questions? If not, then read the story again and continue the lesson. Go back to the questions at the end of the unit. Perhaps you will have answers then.

 Learn the New Words

Here are some of the new words and meanings in this reading.

1. to **assemble** (verb): to put pieces together into a whole thing
2. **blood pressure** (non-count noun): measurement of blood inside veins and arteries; a measure of general health
3. a **cable** (noun): a group of wires together with a plastic cover, used to connect things
4. a **campus** (noun): a place of a college or university, usually with trees and grass between the buildings
5. a **challenge** (noun): a problem to solve
6. to **discard** (verb): to throw away as garbage
7. an **engineer** (noun): a scientist who uses principles to do work of some kind; a type of designer
8. **flow** (non-count noun): movement of things from one stage to another; process
9. a **gadget** (noun): a small machine to do a job, such as open cans, wash dishes, or pump up a tire
10. a **greenhouse** (noun): a house of glass especially made to grow plants under controlled conditions
11. a **jumble** (noun): a disorganized collection of things
12. **junk** (non-count noun): useless things; things to throw away
13. to **keep a record** (verb): to write down progress; to keep a schedule
14. to **limit** (verb): to control; to put a stop to
15. **oxygen** (non-count noun): the part of air that people need to breathe
16. a **prototype:** a model; a working sample, usually smaller than the original

17. a **request** (noun): something that someone asks for

18. **research** (non-count noun): study with a focus to improve or learn from; experiments

19. a **shield** (noun): a protective cover

20. to **sniff out** (verb): to use one's nose (or instincts) to find something

21. a **storehouse** (noun): a place to store supplies

22. a **tube** (noun): a small hose; a long piece of plastic or rubber with a hole in the middle through which a liquid or gas can run

Practice the New Words

A. Look at the list of new words. Which new words answer these questions?

1. Where can you grow plants in the winter? _____

2. What is a difficult problem to solve? _____

3. What word means "all the little tools in a kitchen"?

_____

4. What kind of chart shows a whole process, from start to finish?

_____ chart

5. Which word is like a small hose that can carry water?

_____

6. Almost everyone has some useless stuff. What do we call it?

_____

7. If you write down all the money you spent, what are you keeping? _____

8. What part of air do people need to breathe?

_____

9. What do we call a person like Charlie who makes things work?

   _____

10. What do we call doing experiments to learn new things?

   _____

B. Use the new words from the list to complete these sentences. Use the context to figure out which word to use.

1. There was too much sunlight going into the greenhouse, so the engineers made a _____ to _____ the amount of light.

2. A researcher needed something to measure how much air a person needed on a bicycle. He gave this _____ to Charlie and Greg, and three days later he was able to look at a _____ . He said that the model would work.

3. The engineer found a motor that someone had tried to repair. He _____ all the parts and now has a working motor.

4. It is important to have some kind of order in a storehouse, or else it is all a _____ .

5. A dog _____ food.

6. The _____ of the university is a beautiful place, with places for people to work and play.

C. Draw a line between the two words or phrases with similar meanings.

1. tube	a. supply room
2. prototype	b. air
3. junk	c. cable
4. throw away	d. little machine
5. wire	e. hose
6. research	f. find
7. storehouse	g. model
8. sniff out	h. discard
9. gadget	i. jumble
10. oxygen	j. experiments

Find the Details

Skim and scan to find the answers to these questions.

1. Who is Greg Florian? _____

2. How much does Charlie charge for his work? _____

3. Why does Charlie hate to buy anything? _____

4. Where do most researchers get their gadgets? _____

5. Why did Charlie and Greg build a model for treating wastewater?

   _____

6. Why did they need to make a greenhouse shield?

   _____

7. Who does research at the university? _____

8. How much money has Charlie saved researchers?

   _____

9. How many projects had Charlie completed in nine years?

   _____

10. What kinds of things does Charlie collect? _____

Give Your Opinion

Read these questions. Tell your classmates what you think.

1. Why is a thing junk to one person and not another?
2. How do you feel about new and used things? Which do you prefer? Why?
3. How is what Charlie does good for the environment?

Make Some Inferences

Read and think about these questions. Then try to answer them.

1. Here are some proverbs, or sayings. Can you explain what they mean?

   "Junk is something that you throw away two weeks before you need it."

   "One man's wish is another man's poison."

   "You can't make a silk purse out of a sow's ear."

2. Why do you think Charlie makes prototypes before he makes the machines?
3. What kind of research would require a blood pressure cuff for a frog?
4. An engineer like Charlie can save a university a lot of money. Explain how.
5. What does too much sunshine do to plants? What does too little sunshine mean to plants?

Find the Main Ideas

Circle all the right answers.

1. What is the main idea of Charlie Britton's science lab?
   a. We can make it cheaper than you can buy it.
   b. If we collect enough junk, we will have one of everything.
   c. Tell us what you want.
   d. Junk is really a resource.

e. We can use discarded things to make new tools.

f. We fix broken things.

2. What is the main idea of this reading?

   a. A university needs an engineer like Charlie.

   b. No one should have to use junk.

   c. Understanding flow is an important characteristic of an engineer.

   d. Charlie Britton has saved $350,000 and a lot of time in nine years.

3. Which title fits best?

   a. A Master Engineer at a University

   b. A University Researcher

   c. An Unusual Record

   d. A Junk Collector with a Purpose

Write Your Thoughts

1. With your classmates, make a list of pieces of junk. Then choose one thing and find a new use for it.

2. The slogan, or saying, for keeping the environment clean is this: "Reduce, reuse, recycle."

   a. Write how Charlie Britton is a good environmentalist.

   b. Discuss what each of the three words in the slogan means.

   c. Give examples of how you reduce waste, reuse something, and recycle items.

   d. Give your opinion on being kind to the environment by making old things into new things.

18 The Soap Sisters

The Monroe sisters are expert soap-makers.

Prepare to Read

- Do you get any ideas from the title?
- Look at the picture on the first page of this unit. What will you learn about?
- Who are these people?
- Make a list of your own new words, and try to understand the main ideas.

Which words will you probably see in this unit? Circle them.

soap   children   mother   father   farm   washing

sisters   business   books   school   lions   working

Answer These Questions

First read the story, and then try to answer these questions.

1. Who are the soap sisters?
2. How did they get their name?
3. Where do they live?
4. Why did they start making soap?
5. What do they do with their soap now?

Read the Story

The Soap Sisters

1   Hannah, Rachel, and Sarah Monroe make soap. Their parents, Gina and Randy Monroe, are part of the soap-making business too. How did it happen? Well, it's a nice story. Gina and Randy met and got married in California, but they wanted

5   to raise their family in a rural area. They worked and saved for their dream ranch. Finally they found it: a small piece of land of 20 acres, in the Wynoche Valley near Montesano, Washington. The land was overgrown with weeds and bushes, but the Monroes have never feared work. Besides, the farm

10   was close to town and the price was right.

The Monroes wanted to be independent people. Part of their goal is to grow their own food. So after they bought the farm, they went to work on it. First they cleared the land for some buildings. They cleared space for a house, a garden, a

15 greenhouse, a barn, and a chicken coop. They also cleaned up a large open area for a hayfield. And they started building. Now they grow most of their own food. They have a big garden, 15 meters by 6 meters. They have a greenhouse, too. And they raise goats. They have ten of them, and each goat

20 is a member of the family. The three girls, ages 10, 12, and 16, are responsible for the goats. They have to milk the goats twice every day. Together they use the milk to make cheese, butter, and yogurt. They also use goat's milk to make soap.

How did they start making soap? Well, it started with a

25 magazine article. At first they tried it just to make some soap for themselves. Through trial and error, they came upon a perfect recipe. They joke about using all the "errors," the early mistakes that they made with the soap. Now, however, they know the process very well. Each member of the family

30 does part of the job. It's Sarah's job to mix the ingredients. It takes her several hours to get everything ready. She and her mother heat the alkaline- and acid-based parts of the recipe to the exact temperature. They add vegetable oil and goat's milk. Fragrances, all natural, go into the mixture too. Then

35 they mix it gently—they don't want any bubbles. When the thickness is "just right," they pour it into a wooden box with plastic inside it. They leave it on a shelf to cool.

A day later, Randy cuts the block of soap into bars. At this point it is like a big block of cheese. Then he trims the

40 bars so that they are the right shape. The soap is still soft enough for him to put on a stamp, like a brand. The stamp reads, "Three Sisters Soap." The bars then sit for four weeks

45 on a board to dry and harden. Gina explains that soap gets harder and milder as it sits and dries. Three Sisters Soap is very mild. It is only slightly alkaline. It is nearly neutral, and certainly less alkaline than factory-made soaps.

The three girls wrap each bar of soap by hand. They put the bars in boxes to send to the stores that sell it. There are a dozen local stores that handle it, and more goes to California, 50 Utah, and Tennessee. The price is $2.99 a bar.

The first year in business, they made 600 bars of soap. The second year, they made 1,500 bars. And each year the number increases. The holiday season, from October to December, is the busiest time of the year. Many people like 55 to give gifts of really special soap. And that's what the Monroes make. You can buy Milk and Honey soap, Lemon Cream soap, and Tangerine Cream. They all smell good, and they are very gentle. They are like the mild and gentle people who make the soap, the three sisters and their parents.

Now go back to *Answer These Questions.*

Can you answer the questions? If not, then read the story again and continue the lesson. Go back to the questions at the end of the unit. Perhaps you will have answers then.

Learn the New Words

Here are some of the new words and meanings in this reading.

1. **acid** (adjective and noun): sharp in taste, a chemical property; or a substance having a pH value lower than 7 (for example, vinegar is an acid, and oranges and tomatoes have acid in them)

2. **alkaline** (adjective and noun): salty in taste, a chemical property; or a substance having a pH value higher than 7 (for example, salt, celery, and potato chips are all alkaline in taste)

3. **-based** (combining form): having an origin or foundation in (for example, an acid-based substance is built on an acid)

4. a **block** (noun): a chunk, like a large brick or a large piece of cheese

5. **bubbles** (noun plural): air-filled soap film; air pockets

6. a **chicken coop** (noun): a structure or shelter for poultry; a place for nesting and laying eggs

7. to **clear land** (idiom): to cut down trees and cut away bushes and weeds; to prepare land for growing crops or buildings

8. a **fragrance** (noun): a pleasant smell

9. **gently** (adverb): carefully; smoothly; kindly

10. a **greenhouse** (noun): a glass structure in which plants can grow even in cold weather

11. to **handle** (verb): when referring to a business, to buy and sell for a supplier

12. the **holiday season** (idiom, noun): the period of time from late November until early January, including Thanksgiving, Hanukkah, Christmas, Kwanzaa, New Year's Eve, and New Year's Day

13. an **ingredient** (noun): any food item in a recipe

14. **mild** (adjective): not strong; gentle

15. **neutral** (adjective): neither acid not alkaline; having a pH of 7

16. **overgrown** (adjective): wild and full of weeds

17. a **process** (noun): a series of steps in making something

18. a **recipe** (noun): a series of instructions and ingredients for making something, usually something to eat

19. **rural** (adjective): not of the city; of the countryside; related to farms

20. a **stamp** (noun): a mark; a brand

21. **trial and error** (idiom): the process of trying or testing many of the possible ways of doing something and making each attempt better than the last

22. to **trim** (verb): to cut the edges of a rough surface so that the surface is smooth

23. **weeds** (noun plural): wild plants that interfere with farming

24. to **wrap** (verb): to cover the outside of with paper

Practice the New Words

A. Look at the list of new words. Which new words answer these
   questions?

   1. Which of the new words are names for structures?

   _____ _____ _____

   2. Which three words are about chemical composition?

   _____ _____ _____

   3. What is the opposite of *roughly*? _____

   4. What causes something to be overgrown? _____

   5. What word describes something that is not acid and not
      alkaline? _____

   6. What word describes a farming region? _____

B. Use the new words from the list to complete these sentences. Use
   the context to figure out which word to use.

   1. A really good soap is _____ , and it has a pleasant

      _____ .

   2. To make a field out of an _____ field, one must

      _____ by removing bushes and _____ .

   3. Life in the city is usually busy, but _____ life is
      usually more peaceful.

   4. I have a good _____ for chocolate cake. It has

      tomato soup in it as one of its _____ .

   5. Stores sell a lot of fancy paper during the _____

      because people use it to _____ gifts for others.

6. Mr. Monroe cuts the big _____ of soap, and one

   of the girls _____ the edges to make nice bars of

   soap.

7. The soap is soft, so a _____ with the name

   "Three Sisters" can be put on top.

8. Children like to play with soap because they enjoy seeing

   _____ in the air.

9. The Monroe family's soap-making business is a home

   industry. (It is a home _____ business.)

10. Their recipe is perfect now because they used the

   _____ of _____ .

11. The Monroes send boxes of soap to stores that _____

   it for them.

12. The weather was not cold and stormy. In fact, it was

   _____ for December.

C. Draw a line between the two related words or phrases.

1. fragrance	a. chemical composition
2. neutral	b. brand
3. block	c. not of the city
4. recipe	d. cover
5. stamp	e. gentle
6. mild	f. neither acid nor alkaline
7. weeds	g. smell
8. acid	h. large piece
9. rural	i. overgrown
10. wrap	j. instructions for a process

D. Match a verb from the numbered list with a noun or noun phrase from the other list.

1. mix		a. animals
2. raise		b. a fragrance
3. grow		c. the edges
4. clear		d. a package
5. wrap		e. ingredients
6. handle		f. vegetables
7. smell		g land
8. trim		h. business

Find the Details

Skim and scan to find the answers to these questions.

1. Who are Hannah, Rachel, and Sarah Monroe?

   _____

2. What buildings did the Monroes put on their land?

   _____

3. Which buildings are for animals?   _____

4. How large is their farm? How large is their garden?

   _____ _____

5. What is their goal on their farm?   _____

6. Where is their farm?   _____

7. Why do the Monroes have a lot of milk?   _____

8. How often must a goat be milked?   _____

9. What do the Monroes do with all the milk?

   _____

10. What kind of people are the Monroes?   _____

Give Your Opinion

Read these questions. Tell your classmates what you think.

1. Do the Monroes make a lot of money making soap?
2. What do you think of people who want to make everything for themselves and grow their own food?
3. What is your opinion of homemade foods?
4. Which is better, made in a factory or made at home?
5. The goal of the Monroes is to be "self-sufficient." That means that they want to make for themselves what they can and not have to depend on others. Talk about other people who believe this way. What kind of people are they? Is the Monroes' goal a good one? Why or why not?

Make Some Inferences

Read and think about these questions. Then try to answer them.

1. What are some things a person can make out of milk?

   _____

2. How can one avoid getting bubbles in a bar of soap?

   _____

3. Why is it good for soap to sit on a shelf for a long time before it is wrapped? _____

4. What does this statement mean? "The price was right."

   _____

5. What is a farm-based home? _____

6. What is a home-based business? _____

Find the Main Ideas

Circle all the right answers.

1. What is the main idea of the Monroes' farm?
    a. A piece of land is necessary for every person.
    b. It is good to grow one's own food.
    c. A family should work together and learn to cooperate.
    d. Use the things that you have to make the things that you need.
    e. Every person in a family should help the whole family.
    f. Working together is fun.

2. What is the main idea behind a good business?
    a. Everyone needs soap.
    b. If you have a good product, then you can find customers to buy it.
    c. A farm is a good place to have a home-based business.
    d. There must be one person who runs the business.
    e. You should sell only one thing in your business.
    f. Business is good during the holiday season.

Write Your Thoughts

1. With your classmates, make a list of things that are necessary for daily life (food, shelter, water, clothing, soap, and so on). How many of these things can you make yourself? Choose one item and write about the process of making it.

2. Write how you make something. Choose something that you know how to make.

3. Soap that is not acid or alkaline is neutral. Ideas that are neither for nor against are also neutral. Colors that are not bright are also neutral. Can a person be neutral? When? How? Write your answer.

Learning to Speak Klallam

Adeline Smith (on the left) and Bea Charles (her niece, on the right) are elders of the Klallam tribe. They remember the Klallam language, so they made recordings to save their language. Children at Port Angeles School can study Klallam language. The class fulfills the language requirement for college.

The elders of a tribe can teach the young. It is the traditional way for culture to be learned.

Prepare to Read

- Who are the people in the schools? What are they learning?
- Look at the pictures on the first page of this unit. What will you learn about?

Which of these words and ideas will you probably see in this unit? Circle them.

class   teacher   students   animals   language

recipes   singing   customs   alphabets   making things

- Make a list of your own new words, and try to understand the main ideas.
- Do you get any ideas from the title?

Answer These Questions

First read the story, and then try to answer these questions.

1. What is the connection between language and culture?
2. What is a heritage language?
3. What was the purpose of boarding schools?
4. How did linguists save Klallam?
5. Who is Bea Charles? Why is she an important person in the story?
6. Who is Jamie Valadez? Why is she an important person in the story?

Read the Story

Learning to Speak Klallam

1   Urban Indians speak English, and they might not know their own culture. It is part of what happens to them because they live in the city. They learn English because it is everywhere. Members of the Klallam tribe of Olympic
5   Peninsula were no different. During the first half of the 20th century, the people of many native tribes were told to learn

English. Their children were taken to special schools, called boarding schools. They lived in dormitories and went home only a few times a year. The children had to learn English,
10   and sometimes they were punished for speaking their native language. Few people understood that there was a problem. They thought the children would learn English and keep their native language too. But that is not what was happening. English was taking the place of the native languages.

15   In the 1920s and 1930s, many anthropologists warned that languages would be lost. The effort to save languages, however, was not always successful. There were no easy-to-use tape recorders in those days. As the old people of a tribe died, the languages died with them. The cultural variety of
20   the people of North America was shrinking. Then, in the 1990s, a new effort to save the many native languages of American peoples was started. These languages are called "heritage languages."

        It took eight years to start teaching oral Klallam language
25   in the classroom. The work started in 1990. At that time, there were only a few of the old people left. These elders were the only people who could speak Klallam. Five elders were given tape recorders. They were told to talk as long as they wanted to. Some of them talked for hours and hours.
30   They seemed to enjoy it. One woman sat with her uncle through two years of talking. He died, but he was happy that the language would live on. He laughed about it. When he was a child, he couldn't speak Klallam at school. He said, "Now the white man wants us to speak it again."

35   A linguist, a language specialist, was hired to create an alphabet for Klallam. The language had never been written before. Now, with an alphabet, people are able to write down Klallam stories.

40   Preparation for teaching Klallam took time too. The teacher had to learn the language first. Jamie Valadez learned Klallam so that she could teach it at Port Angeles High School. The younger children don't learn the language. First they learn about the culture of the tribe. Because the Klallam lived near the ocean, there was a great deal about the 45   sea in their culture. They were great fishermen, too, with many traditions around fishing. They also had great celebrations. One of their traditions is the potlatch. This very interesting custom is a gift-giving contest. It was a way of making sure that everyone had what he or she needed.

50   Today, schoolchildren make crafts in the old traditions. They make dream-catchers and bracelets, canoes and drums. As they learn about their heritage, they feel better about themselves. Their self-esteem increases, and they hold their heads higher. She says that the children are acting better. 55   They have pride in who they are. They show respect for their heritage.

    Bea Charles worked hard on this project. She is 80 years old. She is one of the elders who worked on transcribing the language. "Transcribing was the worst part," she said. "It 60   was a tedious job to go through the tape, stop, and translate it into English. Sometimes there just wasn't a word to match the meaning in our language."

    Seventeen-year-old James Charles grew up close to the Klallam reserve. However, he is an urban Indian. He grew up 65   away from the rest of the tribe. He had little knowledge of his native culture. James Charles is pleased to be learning about his people. He is learning to speak the Klallam language. He says he will teach his children so the language will live on.

Now go back to *Answer These Questions.*

Can you answer the questions? If not, then read the story again and continue the lesson. Go back to the questions at the end of the unit. Perhaps you will have answers then.

Learn the New Words

Here are some of the new words and meanings in this reading.

1. a **boarding school** (noun): a school at which the students also live and eat

2. a **canoe** (noun): a simple kind of boat, usually made out of tree bark (but modern ones are usually made out of fiberglass or aluminum)

3. a **celebration** (noun): a festival; a time of great excitement because of a happening

4. **crafts** (noun plural): the things that people make for use or decoration

5. a **custom** (noun): a way of life or a way of doing things that is typical of a group of people

6. a **dormitory** (noun): a place where students live in rooms; a student hotel

7. a **dream-catcher** (noun): a Native American symbol that looks like a circle with a decorated web of metal or thread

8. to **hold one's head up high** (idiom): to walk with pride and self-assurance

9. a **linguist** (noun): a person who is a language expert

10. **native** (adjective): born in a place; of a place for many years

11. to **punish** (verb): to discipline for doing something wrong

12. a **reserve** (noun): a separate place of safety, or an extra supply

13. **self-esteem** (non-count noun): positive feelings about one's own efforts

14. to **shrink** (verb): to get smaller

15. to **take the place of** (idiom): to substitute for; to replace

16. **tedious** (adjective): boring; tiring; not exciting

17. to **transcribe** (verb): to write out the words of a recording
18. **tribe** (noun): a group of people who share common background, language, and customs
19. **urban** (adjective): of the city; not rural
20. to **warn** (verb): to tell of a danger; to alert

Practice the New Words

A. Look at the list of new words. Which new words answer these questions?

1. At what kind of school do students live? _____

2. What do we call the things that people make out of trees, wood, clay, cloth, and so on? _____

3. What do we have on special days like holidays?

   _____

4. Which word is a kind of boat? _____

5. At special times of the year, people give gifts to others. What do we call the ways people do things, like giving gifts?

   _____

6. What do we call an area of land that is kept separate for a specific purpose? _____

7. Where do students keep their things, and where do they sleep?

   _____

8. Which of the new words is like a thing for good luck?

   _____

9. What do we call a group of people like the Klallam?

   _____

10. Which word is a person? _____

B. Use the new words from the list to complete these sentences. Use the context to figure out which word to use.

1. Don't wash that sweater in hot water. It might

   _____ .

2. As a gift, the artist made a lovely circle of a

   _____ .

3. If you feel good about yourself, you have _____ .

4. If you are proud of who you are, you _____ .

5. A person who lives in a city is an _____
   dweller.

6. Sewing, knitting, working with leather, and making pottery
   are all old _____ .

7. One way to _____ a person is to put him or her
   in a prison.

8. A bell rang to _____ the people that a train was
   coming into the station.

C. Draw a line between the two related words or phrases.

1.	urban	a. smaller
2.	shrink	b. alert
3.	warn	c. group of people
4.	punish	d. born there
5.	sleep	e. boat
6.	self-esteem	f. way of doing things
7.	canoe	g. not rural
8.	custom	h. discipline
9.	linguist	i. pride
10.	tribe	j. dormitory
11.	native	k. safe, separate place
12.	reserve	l. anthropologist

Find the Details

Skim and scan to find the answers to these questions.

1. Where do urban Indians live? _____

2. What language do urban Indians most likely speak?

   _____

3. When did anthropologists understand the danger to native

   languages? _____

4. How can a language be saved? _____

5. When did the Klallam project begin? _____

6. What is an elder? _____

7. What did the linguist have to make for Klallam? Why?

   _____

8. Why did it take eight years to start teaching Klallam language?

   _____

9. How can people write down Klallam stories now? Why was it not

   possible twenty years ago? _____

10. What is a potlatch?   _____

 Give Your Opinion

Read these questions. Tell your classmates what you think.

1. Do you think it is valuable to learn a language that has only a few speakers?

2. Should students learn languages in schools?

3. How does a language influence a person's way of thinking?

4. For many years, the children from native tribes went to boarding schools to learn English. What is your opinion of these boarding schools? How did boarding schools affect the tribes?

5. What is your opinion of a gift-giving contest?

 Make Some Inferences

Select the best answer.

1. How does a language die?
    a. It dies from old age because younger languages take over.
    b. It dies because the number of speakers gets smaller and smaller.
    c. It dies because anthropologists study it and record it so that others cannot learn it.
    d. It dies because it does not take in new words.

2. What are the strongest influences on an urban Indian in daily life?
    a. business in the native language of the tribe
    b. dealing with other people who speak Klallam
    c. music and conversation on tape recordings
    d. everyday conversations and business in English

3. What are the advantages (positive parts) of being able to speak more than one language?

   a. You can talk more often.

   b. You can speak to everyone.

   c. You can understand things in two ways.

   d. You can become a tourist and travel more.

4. The Klallam tribe lives near the ocean. How has this fact affected Klallam culture?

   a. They fish a lot.

   b. They enjoy water sports.

   c. They build ships.

   d. They have swimming contests.

5. Self-esteem is important to young people because…

   a. people who are proud of who they are behave better.

   b. old traditions make better people.

   c. they can hold their heads up high.

   d. these people really know who they are.

6. Why did a linguist have to help the Klallam project?

   a. Only linguists speak Klallam.

   b. A linguist understands how to create an alphabet.

   c. Klallam is a very difficult language, and only an expert could understand it.

   d. The Klallam elders asked for help in recording the language.

 Find the Main Ideas

Circle all the right answers.

1. The main idea of the oral Klallam language classes is…

   a. that the children could keep their English and learn Klallam too.

   b. that young people of a tribe must learn to speak the language and must use it to save the language and culture.

    c. that tape recorders can be language teachers.

    d. that it is important to keep a lot of different cultures.

    e. that anthropologists need to learn the language.

2. The main idea of the saving of Klallam is that…

    a. a language can die with its old people.

    b. samples of the language can be saved through a tape recorder.

    c. a person may die, but the language can live on.

    d. only anthropologists speak Klallam.

    e. it, like all heritage languages, can be saved from dying out.

Write Your Thoughts

1. What languages do you think are the most important in the world? Why?

2. Do you believe that it is valuable to keep languages?

3. What can you say in one language and not in another? (Why is it true that some languages are smaller than others?)

A Day on a Tall Ship

On board the *Thayer*, children learn about sailing and about following orders.

The children learn about working together.

Prepare to Read

- Look at the pictures on the first page of this unit. What will you learn about?

Which of these ideas will you probably see in this unit? Write a check (✓) in the blank next to each one.

_____ information about traveling on the ocean

_____ information about schools

_____ stories about old sailors

_____ information about learning languages

_____ ideas for getting new jobs

_____ how to learn to cook

_____ ideas about what it is like to be on a ship

_____ stories about building new houses

_____ instructions for building a ship

_____ information about new kinds of school programs

- Make a list of your own new words, and try to understand the main ideas.
- Do you get any more ideas from the title or the picture?

Answer These Questions

First read the story, and then try to answer these questions.

1. What is the Age of Sail program?
2. Where does this story take place?
3. What is the *C. A. Thayer?*
4. What is the captain like?
5. Who are the lads on the ship? What is a crew on a ship?

Read the Story

A Day on a Tall Ship

1   They call it the Age of Sail. For nineteen hours, a group of landlubbers will be a captain's crew aboard the *C. A. Thayer.* This ship was built over 100 years ago. Its purpose was to

carry lumber to California from the Canadian province of
5 British Columbia and from the U.S. states of Washington and
Oregon. Today, this ship and a number of other historic ships
dock at the Hyde Street Pier in San Francisco. The ships are
all part of the National Historic Park. The *Thayer* is an old
ship, and it needs a lot of repair. However, it makes a great
10 classroom for young people. It is the classroom for the Age of
Sail.

The *Thayer* is one of two remaining 19th century lumber
schooners. After the great earthquake of 1906, San Francisco
was in ruins. To rebuild the city, the people needed wood,
15 and lots of it. Five hundred lumber schooners made the trip
to the northern saw mills and returned with lumber. Today's
California cities are built of stronger material than wood, and
there are no more lumber schooners. However, these ships
were an important part of California history.

20 Every year more than 10,000 schoolchildren learn about
living aboard a ship by living on the *Thayer* for 19 hours. The
children, ages 9 to 12, come from all parts of California and
neighboring states. They stay overnight on the ship. The
person in charge is the captain. The captain, the first and
25 second mates, and the cooks are really employees of the
museum. However, they play their ship roles perfectly. They
try to turn landlubbers into sailors.

Some of the parents of the children come along, but they
do not participate in the learning. They watch to make sure
30 that the children are safe. Parents do not talk except in
warning. Meanwhile, the children begin to find out about life
on a ship. They learn how to handle the ropes. They learn to
row a longboat. They have an opportunity to hoist a sail high
into the air. They even have a chance to cook on a small
35 wood-burning stove. It is all part of the Age of Sail program.

When the children arrive, they think the program will be fun. They quickly learn, however, that being on a ship can be hard work, too. The most important lesson on the ship is learning to follow directions. The captain does not tolerate

40   any kind of bad behavior.

A new group of children (they are the "lads") is on board. The lads are excited and noisy, like all children. The captain growls, "Sit like I told you!" They all take notice. "Eat like I told you to eat!" he snaps. And the children stop talking and

45   pick up their forks. The lads must learn to follow orders.

Each class is divided into five separate crews. Each crew has a particular job to perform on the ship. Some of them will work in the ship's kitchen, the galley. They will prepare the meals for the others. They will learn that cooking is not

50   easy on a ship. Other children will work with the ropes and sails. Some will be cleaning the ship. At first the jobs are easy. As the day passes, however, the jobs become more challenging.

The captain calls all the crews together. He says, "Being a sailor is one of the hardest jobs there is. The sea doesn't

55   care if you sink or float. Nobody will slap you harder than the sea." The children learn that he speaks the truth. They learn to work together to finish tough work. They cooperate as they lift heavy pieces of wood. Together they carry things that one person could not carry. They sing to keep the rhythm

60   of the work just like sailors of 100 years ago. But most of all, they learn the importance of obeying the captain and the mates. On a ship, the lads must be able to depend on one another. If one person doesn't follow directions, every other person on board could be in danger.

Now go back to *Answer These Questions.*

Can you answer the questions? If not, then read the story again and continue the lesson. Go back to the questions at the end of the unit. Perhaps you will have answers then.

Learn the New Words

Here are some of the new words and meanings in this reading.

1. **aboard** (adverb): on a ship
2. **on board** (idiom): on a ship
3. **challenging** (adjective): difficult; not easy to do
4. a **crew** (noun): a group of people who work together on one project
5. to **dock** (verb): to tie up a ship in a harbor
6. to **float** (verb): to stay on top of the water
7. a **galley** (noun): a kitchen on a ship or boat
8. to **growl** (verb): to make a sound like a bear; to roar; to talk in a rough voice
9. to **hoist** (verb): to pull up with a rope
10. **in charge** (idiom): the boss; in a position to tell others what to do
11. a **lad** (noun): a young boy (or girl)
12. a **landlubber** (noun): a person who has no experience with sailing
13. a **mate** (noun): a partner; an officer on a ship
14. a **pier** (noun): a place to tie up a ship in a harbor
15. to **play a role** (idiom): to act a part in a play; to pretend
16. a **purpose** (noun): the reason for doing
17. **rhythm** (non-count noun): a musical beat; a steady pace
18. a **schooner** (noun): a sailing ship
19. to **slap** (verb): to hit with one's hand, usually in punishment
20. to **snap** (verb): to give a quick, sharp order; to answer rudely
21. to **take notice** (idiom): to see; to become aware
22. to **tolerate** (verb): to be willing to allow
23. a **warning** (noun): an alert; words that tell of a danger

Practice the New Words

A. Look at the list of new words. Which words from the list answer these questions?

1. Who is in charge of the ship when the captain is asleep?

    _____

2. Where does the cook on a ship work?   _____

3. What do we call making the sound of an angry bear or a dog?

    (Use the *-ing* form of the verb.)   _____

4. In a harbor, where does a ship dock?   _____

5. How do you describe a job that is really too hard for you?

    _____

6. What are the children in the Age of Sail program called?

    _____

B. Use the new words from the list to complete these sentences. Use the context to figure out which word to use.

1. On the schooner, there are some large white rings. These rings,

    lifesavers, will _____ on the surface. Something
    heavier might sink to the bottom.

2. The first mate has a kind voice, but the captain _____
    his orders.

3. One kind of music is a waltz. It has a 1-2-3 _____ .

4. That man is no sailor. He's a _____ !

5. What time can we go _____ the ship? I am

    glad that we are going _____ *(2 words)* that

    ship. It will _____ at the _____

    at five o'clock.

6. The captain has a good first _____ and a good

   _____ of twenty men.

7. These people are employees of the museum, but they

   _____ as captain and mates well.

8. A good captain has strong discipline. He does not

   _____ bad behavior at all.

9. The small boy hid in the galley, and no one _____
   of him until the ship had left the harbor.

10. The captain spoke sharply. He _____ , "I told
    you to sit down and eat!"

11. The captain is _____ of the ship.

12. What is the _____ of so many sails? Why do
    we have so many?

C. Draw a line between the two related words or phrases.

1. growl	a. first and second mate
2. galley	b. beat in music
3. hoist	c. look
4. captain	d. snap
5. take notice	e. stand for or allow
6. tolerate	f. kitchen
7. sailors	g. pull up
8. rhythm	h. dock
9. schooner	i. person in charge
10. pier	j. ship

Find the Details

Skim and scan to find the answers to these questions.

1. What is the most important lesson on a ship? _____

2. Who are the captain and his mates in real life? _____

3. What happened in San Francisco in 1906? _____

4. What are California's cities made of now? _____

5. How long does the Age of Sail program last? _____

6. How old are the children who come to stay overnight on the

   Thayer? _____

7. How many schooners carried lumber to California in the early

   1900s? _____

8. Where does the cook make dinner on a schooner?

   _____

9. Why do parents come on board the *Thayer*? _____

10. What is wood for building called? _____

Give Your Opinion

Read these questions. Tell your classmates what you think.

1. Do you think that the Age of Sail is a good program? Why or why not?

2. Do you think a captain should be more tolerant of children's behavior?

3. The *Thayer* is an old ship in need of repair. Should someone spend the money to fix it?

4. Is discipline an important lesson? How does it compare to lessons like working together?

5. Do you think that programs like the Age of Sail are valuable? Why or why not?

6. Would you enjoy a day on a tall ship? Why or why not?

7. Would the program be better if the ship went out to sea? Why or why not?

 Find the Main Ideas

Circle all the correct answers.

1. Which of the following are lessons that children learn on the *Thayer*?

   a. to read books

   b. to handle ropes

   c. to hoist a sail

   d. to follow orders

   e. to cook on a wood-burning stove

   f. to row a longboat

   g. to speak another language

   h. to cut wood into lumber

   i. to listen to the person in charge

2. What is the main idea of the Age of Sail program? (Choose one answer.)

   a. Parents cannot teach their children all the lessons of life.

   b. There is a museum at the National Historic Park.

   c. Children think they will have fun on the *Thayer*.

   d. Children learn some discipline in one day on a schooner.

3. What is the main idea of discipline on a ship? (Choose one answer.)

   a. A person who does not follow orders puts everyone else in danger.

   b. A person who likes to cook would be happy in the galley.

   c. The ship has five main types of work for the lads to do.

   d. The captain and first mate are the two most important people on the ship.

Make Some Inferences

Select the best answer.

1. What makes a ship a tall ship?
   a. the lumber
   b. the sails
   c. the flag
   d. the ship itself

2. When was the *Thayer* built?
   a. more than 100 years ago
   b. in 1906
   c. in 1990
   d. in 1945

3. Where is Hyde Street?
   a. near many schools
   b. not in California
   c. near the harbor
   d. in British Columbia

4. What does the captain mean by these words: "Nobody will slap you harder than the sea."?
   a. The sea is not a person.
   b. The sea will not be difficult for you to handle.
   c. You have to follow the orders of the ocean.
   d. Be foolish and the sea will hurt you.

5. How does one person's good work (or bad work) affect everyone else on a ship?
   a. One person can make a mistake.
   b. Everyone on a ship depends on everyone else for safety.
   c. Ships get old very quickly.
   d. If one person does a good job, others might too.

6. How can children do the hard work of real sailors?
   a. by pretending to be on a ship
   b. by planning how to work together to accomplish important ship tasks
   c. by working together and cooperating
   d. through trial and error

7. Why are ropes important on a ship?
   a. Sailors use ropes to tie things down so they don't float away.
   b. Sailors use the ship's ropes for hanging laundry.
   c. Ropes give sailors something to do.
   d. Ropes hold the sails of the ship.

8. There are many "shanties," or sailors' songs. They all have a very strong rhythm to them. Why do you think they have a strong rhythm?
   a. Sailors like to work and to sing songs while they work.
   b. Sailors love a piece of music with a strong rhythm.
   c. Sailors use the music to work together in rhythm.
   d. Sailors are tough people, so they don't like waltzes.

9. What makes a longboat go forward through the water?
   a. a motor
   b. the rowing of sailors
   c. the wind in the sails
   d. the moving ocean current

10. What makes a schooner go forward through the water?
   a. a motor
   b. the rowing of sailors
   c. the wind in the sails
   d. the moving ocean current

Write Your Thoughts

1. A person can learn a great number of lessons in real life experiences. Think of an experience from your own life that helped you in learning important lessons. Then write about the experience and what you learned from it.

2. Why is discipline so important on a ship? Explain your thoughts.

3. One parent said, "The hardest job of a parent is to let your children make their own mistakes." Do you agree with this statement? At what point would you (as a parent) stop what is happening and take charge?

Word List

A

to abandon (verb) 7
aboard (adverb) 20
academy (noun) 11
acid (noun) 18
acre (noun) 3
adventuresome (adjective) 1
agreement (noun) 10
aircraft (non-count noun) 8
alkaline (adjective) 18
alligator (noun) 12
amateur (noun) 16
to analyze (verb) 4
ancient (adjective) 6
antique (noun) 13
Appalachia (noun) 14
architect (noun) 2
argument (noun) 16
artist (noun) 5
to assemble (verb) 17
to attract (verb) 4
ax (noun) 8

B

balanced (adjective) 7
barge (noun) 13
basin (noun) 1
battery (noun) 10
battle (noun) 10
bay (noun) 6
beach (noun) 7
beak (noun) 15
to be alive and well (idiom) 14
to be extinct (idiom) 9
to be in order (idiom) 8
belongings (noun) 3
better than average (idiom) 11
birdwatcher (noun) 15

block (noun) 18
blood pressure (noun) 17
on board (idiom) 20
boarding (adjective) 19
to border (verb) 13
to bother (verb) 13
to break (noun, verb) 8, 11
bubbles (noun plural) 18
bucket (noun) 1
budget (noun) 12
to build character (idiom) 11
bulldozer (noun) 8
to burrow (verb) 5

C

cable (noun) 13
campus (noun) 17
canoe (noun) 7
carpenter (noun) 2
celebration (noun) 19
cell phone (noun) 3
chain saw (noun) 8
challenge (noun) 11
challenging (adjective) 20
characteristics (noun plural) 9
chemical composition (noun) 5
chicken coop (noun) 18
chimney (noun) 1
choir (noun) 2
choir loft (noun) 2
chunk (noun) 5
to circumnavigate (verb) 16
a classical education (idiom) 11
clear (adjective) 1
climate (noun) 1
clone (noun) 9
clue (noun) 5
coast (noun) 6

collapsible (adjective) 3
colony (noun) 16
to communicate (verb) 12
to concern (noun, verb) 7, 9
to confuse (verb) 16
to connect (verb) 5
to contain (verb) 4
contest (noun) 14
contestant (noun) 14
convent (noun) 2
costume designer (noun) 12
counselor (noun) 11
cove (noun) 16
coyote (noun) 1
crafts (noun plural) 19
creature (noun) 7
crew (noun) 8
crown fire (noun) 8
curious (adjective) 7
custom (noun) 19
cute (adjective) 15
cystic fibrosis (noun) 9

 D

daily (adverb) 11
to date (verb) 6
to deal with (idiom) 12
to decorate (verb) 6
dense (adjective) 13
detective (noun) 6
diameter (noun) 1
dime (noun) 15
dirt track (noun) 1
to discard (verb) 17
disabled (adjective) 14
to disagree (verb) 7
disaster (noun) 6
discipline (noun) 11

to display (verb) 15
to dissolve (verb) 4
ditch (noun) 8
diving (noun) 13
DNA testing (noun) 3
to dock (verb) 20
dolphin (noun) 7
donation (noun) 12
dormitory (noun) 19
drama (noun) 6
dream-catcher (noun) 19
to drive cattle (verb) 3
drug (noun) 9

E

eco-terrorist (noun) 10
emotional (adjective) 4
emotionally (adverb) 4
engineer (noun) 17
to entertain (noun) 14
entertainment industry (noun) 12
enthusiastic (adjective) 15
environmentalist (noun) 10
to erupt (verb) 6
event (noun) 14
evidence (non-count noun) 6
to exercise (verb) 10
to exist (verb) 6
to explode (verb) 8
exotic (adjective) 12
eyebolt (noun) 13
exquisite (adjective) 5
to extinguish (verb) 8

F

faith (noun) 2
fake (noun) 16
feeder (noun) 15

to feel good (idiom) 16
fertilized (adjective) 9
to figure out (idiom) 6
filter (noun) 4
fire and energy (idiom) 11
fit (adjective) 10
flame (noun) 1
flame-retardant (noun) 8
flesh (noun) 9
to float (verb) 13
flow (noun) 17
fluffy (adjective) 1
fluorescent (adjective) 9
foggy (adjective) 10
foul (adjective) 4
fragrance (noun) 18
to freeze/froze (verb) 9
frozen (adjective) 8
fuel break (noun) 8
fund-raiser (noun) 12

 G

gadget (noun) 17
to gain (verb) 15
galley (noun) 20
genetic (adjective) 9
gently (adverb) 18
to give something up (idiom) 12
glaze (noun) 5
graduate (noun) 11
to graze (verb) 3
greenhouse (noun) 17
to growl (verb) 20

 H

hammer (noun) 2
hammock (noun) 1
by hand (idiom) 18

to handle (verb) 13
to hang out with (idiom) 7
harbor (noun) 6
harbor seal (noun) 7
hardwood (noun) 13
to hatch (verb) 7
to have a knack (idiom) 14
to have a twinkle in one's eye
    (idiom) 14
a hero (noun) 14
to hoist (verb) 20
to hold one's head up high
    (idiom) 19
helicopter (noun) 8
herd (noun) 3
heritage (noun) 2
hide (noun) 3
history buff (noun) 16
to holler (verb) 14
to hop (verb) 7
hose (noun) 8
to hover (verb) 8
huge (adjective) 3
hummer (noun) 15
hummingbird (noun) 15

 I

identity (noun) 2
to ignite (verb) 8
in charge (idiom) 20
to increase (verb) 4
ingredient (noun) 18
inlet (noun) 7
inner-city (adjective) 11
inner tube (noun) 13
in ruins (idiom) 6
inspector (noun) 3
inspiring (adjective) 14

intact (adjective) 6
to interview (verb) 10
to investigate (verb) 4

J

jewelry (noun) 5
jigsaw puzzle (noun) 16
joke (noun) 14
jumble (noun) 17
junk (noun) 17

K

kayak (noun) 7
kayaker (noun) 7
to keep alive (idiom) 14
to keep a record (idiom) 17
to keep one's distance (idiom) 7
keyboarding (noun) 11
kiln (noun) 13
lad (noun) 20
ladder (noun) 2
landing (noun) 16
landlubber (noun) 20
lantern (noun) 1
latitude (noun) 16

L

leash (noun) 12
legend (noun) 2
liar (noun) 14
to lie (verb) 6
lie (noun) 14
to limit (verb) 17
limited (adjective) 13
linguist (noun) 19
lively (adjective) 14

location (noun) 6
logger (noun) 13
lumber (non-count noun) 2
lungs (noun plural) 4

M

magnetic waves (noun plural) 6
magnificent (adjective) 2
to make sense out of (idiom) 14
mammoth (noun) 9
maple (noun) 13
mate (noun) 20
mature (adjective) 3
mention (verb) 5
merchandise (noun) 3
metal plate (noun) 16
method (noun) 11
mice (noun plural) 9
microclimate (noun) 8
mild (adjective) 18
mill (noun) 13
mineral (noun) 5
miracle (noun) 2
mist (noun) 10
mucus (non-count noun) 4
mudslide (noun) 10
mystery (noun) 2

N

native (adjective) 2
native people (noun plural) 5
nature (noun) 10
nectar (noun) 15
nerve (noun) 4
neutral (adjective) 18
nickel (noun) 15
non-profit business (idiom) 11

novena (noun) 2
nucleus (noun) 9

 O

oak (noun) 13
obviously (adverb) 13
octagon (noun) 1
old-growth (adjective) 10
opportunity (noun) 7
orangutan (noun) 12
ore (noun) 5
outhouse (noun) 1
out in the open (idiom) 3
to outwit (verb) 14
oven (noun) 13
overgrown (adjective) 18
oxygen (noun) 13

P

paid staff (noun plural) 12
particle (noun) 4
peanut butter (noun) 4
peg (noun) 2
phenomenon (noun) 4
pier (noun) 20
pilgrim (noun) 6
pilgrimage (noun) 6
pirate (noun) 16
plateau (noun) 1
to play a role (idiom) 20
plenty (noun) 13
prayer (noun) 2
precisely (adverb) 8
prison (noun) 11
to polish (verb) 5
pottery (noun) 5
power (noun) 15
precious (adjective) 5

pro (noun) 7
process (noun) 17
prospector (noun) 5
prototype (noun) 17
to punish (verb) 19
pup (noun) 7
puppy (noun) 12
purpose (noun) 4
push-up (noun) 10

R

raft (noun) 13
to raise cattle (idiom) 3
rare (adjective) 2
reaction (noun) 4
recipe (noun) 18
records (noun plural) 16
red-faced (adjective) 14
refuge (noun) 12
to replace (verb) 9
request (noun) 17
to rescue (verb) 7
research (noun) 7
to resemble (verb) 9
reserve (noun) 19
resident (noun) 14
to respond (verb) 4
retired (adjective) 12
revolution (noun) 15
reward (noun) 11
rhythm (noun) 20
to roam (verb) 3
role (noun) 4
to round up (idiom) 3
route (noun) 15
rubble (noun) 5
rural (adjective) 18
rustler (noun) 3

S

sail (noun) 16
satellite communication (noun) 3
sauna (noun) 1
saw (noun) 2
scary (adjective) 14
schooner (noun) 20
seam of ore (noun) 5
seaport (noun) 6
secret (noun) 16
self-esteem (noun) 19
sense (noun) 2
shame (noun) 16
shelter (noun) 12
shield (noun) 17
shrill (adjective) 15
to shrink (verb) 19
signature (noun) 10
simultaneously (adverb) 5
sit-up (noun) 10
skill (noun) 9
to slap (verb) 20
to slide (verb) 10
slope (noun) 8
a snack (noun) 15
to snap (verb) 20
to sniff out (idiom) 17
soil (noun) 4
soldier (noun) 14
solo (adjective) 7
sonar (noun) 13
spider web (noun) 5
spiral (noun) 2
sponge bath (noun) 10
square (adjective) 10
to squeal (verb) 15
stack (noun) 1
stamp (noun) 13

stand (noun) 10
standing-room-only (adjective) 14
steep (adjective) 8
stele (noun) 6
storehouse (noun) 17
strategy (noun) 3
stressful (adjective) 12
to stretch (verb) 3
to substitute (verb) 9
to sum up (idiom) 3
surface (noun) 5237
survival (noun) 15
sweat lodge (noun) 1
to swoop down (idiom) 15

T

tack (noun) 15
tailings (noun plural) 5
to take in (verb) 4
to take notice (idiom) 20
to take the place of (idiom) 19
tale (noun) 14
tanker (noun) 8
tarp (noun) 10
tedious (adjective) 19
terrifying (adjective) 15
theory (noun) 5
to tip over (idiom) 7
to tolerate (verb) 11
tour (noun) 12
to train (verb) 4
to transcribe (verb) 19
trial and error (idiom) 18
tribe (noun) 5
to trim (verb) 18
troublemaker (noun) 11
T square (noun) 2
tub (noun) 2

tube (noun) 17
to twist (verb) 1
twisted (adjective) 1

U

unique (adjective) 1
unstable (adjective) 7
upset (adjective) 12
urban (adjective) 19

V

van (noun) 12
to vanish (verb) 6
vein (noun) 5
visibility (noun) 13
volcanic activity (noun) 5
volcano (noun) 5
voyage (noun) 16
vulnerable (adjective) 3

W

to wander (verb) 3
warehouse (noun) 13
to warn (verb) 19
warning (noun) 4
water-logged (adjective) 13
waterproof (adjective) 1
wattle (noun) 1
waystation (noun) 12
weeds (noun plural) 18
wetness (non-count noun) 4
whale (noun) 7
wheelchair (noun) 14
to whet (verb) 4
whopper (noun) 14
wick (noun) 1

wildlands (noun plural) 8
wildlife (noun) 7
wolves (noun plural) 12
woolly (adjective) 9
to wonder (verb) 7
to be worth (idiom) 1
to wrap (verb) 18

Z

zoologist (noun) 7